Perspectives on Teaching Innovations:
World and Global History

In this series:

Perspectives on Teaching Innovations: World and Global History

a collection of essays from *Perspectives,* the newsletter
of the American Historical Association

with an introduction by Robert Blackey

American Historical Association
Washington, D.C.

AHA Editor: Susan W. Gillespie

Published in 1999 by the American Historical Association. As publisher, the American Historical Association does not adopt official views on any field of history and does not necessarily agree or disagree with the views expressed in this book.

Library of Congress Cataloging-in-Publication Data

Perspectives on teaching innovations : world and global history : a collection of essays from *Perspectives,* the newsletter of the American Historical Association / with an introduction by Robert A. Blackey.
    p. cm.
Originally published: 1989–1998.
Includes bibliographical references.
ISBN 0-87229-112-X
    1. History—Methodology. 2. History—Study and teaching (Secondary)—United States. I. American Historical Association. II. *Perspectives* (Washington, D.C. : 1984)
    D16.P42 1999
    907.1'273-dc21   99-29362
                                                  CIP

Printed in the United States of America

Contents

About the Contributors

Joel Beinin is a professor of Middle East history at Stanford University. Sabine MacCormack, Mary Louise Pratt, Renato I. Rosaldo Jr., Susan A. Stephens, Ann Swidler, David E. Wellbery, the late John Winkler, and Morris Zelditch Jr.—all of whom taught in Conflict and Change in Western Culture—contributed to the ideas in this essay in ways that make individual attribution impossible.

Robert Blackey is a professor of history at California State University, San Bernardino, where he teaches world history and a variety of courses in British and European history. He has been active in the Advanced Placement program for thirty years, most notably as chief reader and as chair of the Test Development Committee for European History. He has served as vice president of the AHA's Teaching Division, and for almost fifteen years edited the Teaching Innovations column in *Perspectives*, in which several of these essays originally appeared. In 1999 he received the Distinguished Service Award from the Western Regional Council of the College Board.

Thomas W. Davis is a professor of history at the Virginia Military Institute, where he has taught since 1972. In addition to teaching and service awards from his college, he has won grants from the American Philosophical Society, the National Endowment for the Humanities, and the Danforth Foundation. His research interest is Britain during the reign of George III; his publications on English Dissenters include one book published by the London Record Society.

Michael F. Doyle is an associate professor of history and the Honors Director at Ocean County College, Toms River, New Jersey. He thanks Lynn Hunt (Univ. of Pennsylvania) and William G. Shade and Mike Baylor (Lehigh Univ.) for reading drafts of the article and for encouraging him.

Lanny Fields is an associate professor of history at California State University, San Bernardino, where he teaches world civilizations and electives in Chinese, Japanese, East Asian, and Russian history.

James Lance, who is completing his dissertation in African history, was a teaching fellow in The World Outside the West. The Teaching Fellows Program was designed to expose advanced graduate students and postdoctoral fellows to the content of this course in order to help them develop similar courses when they begin their professional career.

William H. McNeill was a professor of history at the University of Chicago, where he taught for forty years and wrote a pioneering study of world history entitled *The Rise of the West: A History of the Human Community* (1963). Retired since 1987, his most recent book is entitled *Keeping Together in Time: Dance and Drill in Human History* (1995).

Colin A. Palmer is a distinguished professor of history at the Graduate School of the City University of New York. His most recent work is *Passageways: An Interpretive History of Black America* (Harcourt, Brace, Jovanovich, 1994).

Richard Roberts is an associate professor of African history and has participated in The World Outside the West since its inception. His paper was originally presented as part of a panel on "Teaching World History" held at the 1989 American Historical Association Pacific Coast Branch meeting, Portland, Oregon.

William F. Sater is an emeritus professor of Latin American history at California State University, Long Beach. A contributor to the *Handbook of Latin American Studies,* he has recently published a general history of Chile and a series of articles in the *Encyclopedia of Latin American History*. He also has a book on the German Influence in the Chilean Army in press.

Tara Sethia is an associate professor of History at California State Polytechnic University at Pomona. She teaches courses on India, South Asia, Southeast Asia, Women in Asia, and a three-course sequence in the history of world civilizations. She also served as a project director of a three-year program, "India and China in Comparative and Global Perspective," for the professional development of K–12 teachers. This program was funded by the National Endowment for the Humanities.

Susan Heilbrunn Shapiro teaches at the University of Chicago

Laboratory Schools. She has taught history for twenty-five years in both middle school and high school.

Peter N. Stearns is dean of the College of Humanities and Social Sciences and Heinz Professor of History at Carnegie Mellon University. He regularly teaches in the first-year world history course. Stearns's most recent book is *Battleground of Desire: The Struggle for Self-Control in 20th-Century America*. He has served as vice president of the AHA's Teaching Division and continues to work on patterns of history teaching and learning.

Theodore H. Von Laue, Jacob Francis Hiatt Professor of History emeritus at Clark University, started in German and European history before specializing in Russian and Soviet studies; he also probed into West African affairs and Chinese life on the way to teaching world history with special emphasis on the twentieth century. He has written many scholarly articles and several books, including *Why Lenin? Why Stalin?* (1964; now *Why Lenin? Why Stalin? Why Gorbachev?* HarperCollins, 1993); *The World Revolution of Westernization: The Twentieth Century in Global Perspective* (Oxford Univ. Press, 1987); and *Faces of a Nation: The Rise and Fall of the Soviet Union, 1917–1991* (Fulcrum Publishing, 1996). His most recent teaching assignment was at Shaanxi Teachers University in Xi'an, China, in fall 1989.

Alan T. Wood is a professor and associate dean at the University of Washington, Bothell. He is a coauthor of the Norton college text *World Civilizations*, and author of *Limits to Autocracy: From Sung Neo-Confucianism to a Doctrine of Political Rights;* and *What Does It Mean to be Human?: Balancing Freedom and Authority in World History.*

Acknowledgments

The American Historical Association wishes to thank the following contributing editors for their role in *Perspectives* over the past two decades, without whom neither the newsletter nor this volume would have been possible.

Robert Blackey, the Teaching Innovations contributing editor for nearly fifteen years, was responsible for soliciting and for the initial editing of the articles by Thomas W. Davis, Lanny Fields, James Lance and Richard Roberts, William H. McNeill, Colin A. Palmer, William F. Sater, Tara Sethia, Peter N. Stearns, and Alan Wood.

As coeditors, Blackey and Howard Shorr contributed the articles by Joel Beinin and Theodore H. Von Laue.

David Trask arranged for *Perspectives* to reprint Michael F. Doyle's article from the *ECCSSA Journal;* the journal has again granted permission to reproduce the article in this volume

Introduction

Awareness of the need for a universal view of history—for a history which transcends national and regional boundaries and comprehends the entire globe—is one of the marks of the present.... Our civilization is the first to have for its past the past of the world, our history is the first to be world history.... And since 1945 the world has moved into a new phase of global integration, the demand for a history which reflects this new situation has become more insistent.

—Geoffrey Barraclough

World history is no more difficult than national history. What one needs is a clear and distinct idea that will define what is relevant.

—William H. McNeill

The throes of the contemporary world are those of a birth. And what is being born with such great pain is a universal human society.... What characterizes the events we witness, what distinguishes them from all preceding events back to the origins of history is...their global character.

—Etienne Gilson

Establishing a central place for world and global history under the umbrella of our discipline and within the halls of educational institutions no longer needs to be defended; indeed, the advice and charges of colleagues such as Barraclough, McNeill, and Gilson, among others, has been heeded with considerable gusto. Not only is there a substantial scholarship growing up around the subject, along with the now well-established World History Association, but there are also National Standards for teaching world history that, in the ominous shadow of a publicly partisan, media-driven national debate, even managed to become oriented globally, thanks in part to the advice and suggestions of the AHA's Task Force and to the other reviewing professional organizations that effectively refined and advanced the initial drafts written under the aegis of the National History Standards Project. In addition, world history is an integral part of the standards and frameworks of many among the fifty states, it is taught alongside or has frequently replaced Western civilization courses in our two- and four-year colleges and universities, it is the focus of a few graduate programs (for example, at Hawaii and Northeastern), and its study has spawned a new generation of world history textbooks with more clearly defined global emphases.

As it was taught in the 1960s and 70s, however—and to the extent that it was taught at all—the typical world history course was usually little more than Western Civ with a few add-ons, like a vacation to Europe that includes a side trip to Morocco. But then the late 1980s and the decade of the 90s brought a revised perspective on world history, a history of the world guided by a global outlook and, in turn, reflective of the post–Cold-War world we live in that is characterized by a new international system called globalization. Thus to increasing numbers of historians, world history is as important as any history we teach.

Preparing to teach world history is a major intellectual challenge. Prospective instructors have to grapple with the interaction between and among civilizations, with the multiplicity of events and people in the long and multifaceted saga of humankind, with themes, trends, and the vagaries of cultural diffusion, and with change and continuity in an array of regions that did not form part of their academic training. For those just starting their world history courses, this pamphlet provides a precious resource and a fund of experience and knowledge that will make a difficult task somewhat easier. For those who have been teaching world history for many years, the pamphlet will initiate further reflection on how best to teach the course and on experimentation with some of the insights suggested by these historians.

Unlike other pamphlets and collections of articles on world and global history—which are mostly aimed at an audience of scholars in, or interested in, the field—the essays you are poised to examine are directed at classroom teachers, both secondary school and college, many of whom are relative novices in the field. One of the themes that is woven throughout these pages is that world history is not simply a reiteration, in summary fashion, of the separate histories of various societies, say of English history plus Chinese history plus Brazilian history, and so on, but rather the study of common themes and experiences and of the interactions between and among civilizations. A related theme is that separate national and regional histories are enhanced when considered in relation to world history. United States history, for example, is traditionally taught as if this nation of immigrants existed apart from the world, except where the world intrudes, say during a world war or an economic crisis or a health emergency. The selection by Peter Stearns demonstrates what is flawed with this approach and suggests ways to remedy it.

Another critical concern, alluded to above, is that world history must not be taught as Western civilization enhanced by a few trinkets and occasional detours to other lands outside the blessed ring formed by Europe, the Mediterranean, and North America, with the civilizations of those strange and unfamiliar places seen only from a Western perspective. The essays by Joel Beinin (on the Middle East), Colin Palmer (on the Caribbean), William Sater and Susan Shapiro (on Latin America), and Tara Sethia (on India) provide a cornucopia of suggestions, including themes, approaches, and readings, to help make any world history course fuller and more global in its approach. [Unfortunately, there are, although not for want of trying, obvious gaps here—including articles on the regions of Africa, on China, Japan, and other major Asian civilizations, on Polynesia—but perhaps these will be forthcoming in future teaching columns in *Perspectives* or in the other teaching journals, *The History Teacher* and *Teaching History: A Journal of Methods*.]

The first of the three sections into which this collection is divided is called *World History or Western Civilization?* with the opening salvo fired by Thomas W. Davis. His "Starting from Scratch: Shifting from Western Civ to World History" serves the dual purpose of providing invaluable direction and practical suggestions for those who are preparing to teach world history for the first time as well as for those making the transition from a Western to a world civilization course. Davis is a teacher who, after a couple of decades at the Western Civ trough, became convinced that a change was in order. He guides us through the stages of this evolution, including his own internal conflicts and what he had to do within his department and university to make it happen; he also tells us what he read, and why, and how his course is structured.

Like Davis, Michael F. Doyle, in "'Hisperanto': Western Civilization in the Global Curriculum," gives careful thought to J. H. Hexter's always-relevant curricular question: What is best for our students? But with regard to this two-sided coin—Western or world history—Doyle's carefully developed arguments lead him to a conclusion different from Davis's. Nevertheless, we see the influence of the debate over these two civ courses when he notes that the Western Civ course of today is likely to be one reflecting a greater global awareness. In addition, he summarizes and evaluates many of the arguments against teaching world history, which even advocates of that course would be wise to consider.

Rounding out this section is Alan Wood's "Freedom in World History: Can Parachutists and Truffle-Hunters Find Happiness Together?" in which he confronts the roles played by generalists and specialists as they relate to the study and teaching of world history. It is his contention "that the broad perspective afforded by the study of the human condition as a whole is complementary and not antithetical to the highly specialized research most of us engage in as professional historians." Further, he argues in favor of the process of synthesis being elevated in the thinking of historians to the same level and value as analysis, and he reminds us that world history—both taught and studied—is the granddaddy of all syntheses. He also argues in favor of reconsidering the development of human freedom as one appropriate organizing principle in world history.

Among the reading suggestions made by Tom Davis there are a number of articles that, at least for me when I first prepared to teach world history, offered invaluable assistance as I conceived and shaped my course, that helped me to envision in my mind's eye what I would be doing before I could begin to organize it in fact. The second section in this collection, *Perspectives on Teaching World History,* offers four essays that are complementary to Davis's select group of readings.

However much notions of the world as a "global village" have become variations on a cliché, the fact remains that the twenty-first-century world is and will be one of interdependence. It is from this perspective that Theodore H. Von Laue, in "A Declaration of Interdependence: World History for the Twenty-First Century," advises us to continue our examination and discussion of world history, but especially from the perspective of cultural diversity ("because we are a culturally diverse nation in a culturally diverse world") and from the realization that growing interdependence is also based upon Western achievements. To be sure, these subjects are fraught with cultural tripwires, but they must be confronted as reflections of reality while, not incidentally, they help to give contemporary meaning and relevance to what our students might otherwise see as a bloated and unmanageable subject. By way of conclusion, Von Laue suggests a broad outline for teaching world history that reflects his previously-stated considerations.

The next three articles in this section were published together as a forum focusing on issues related to the teaching of world history. First, James Lance and Richard Roberts, in "The World Outside the West Course Sequence at Stanford University," dissect Stanford University's non-Western culture requirement, a sequence of two midlevel courses that provides an interdisciplinary and cross-cultural emphasis and is taught by a team of area specialists. These courses are a compromise between the sweep of the traditional world history approach and a kind of postholing in that they examine and compare the cultures of three countries/civilizations, both before and after contact with the West. The goals of these courses include exposing students to ranges of diversity in three different parts of the world and challenging them to think critically about the designated three areas both in relationship to one another and to the West. Although, for various reasons, other universities might not be able or even wish to replicate this Stanford model, the thinking that went into the course sequence, along with the hoped-for goals and problems encountered, offer the rest of us much to reflect upon.

Lanny Fields gives us the benefit of his considered reflection in "Some Thoughts About the Stanford Course The World Outside the West." He particularly takes the organizers of the course sequence to task for a structure that is subtly, but probably unintentionally, Eurocentric in that it appears to reveal "Western-derived or baseline expectations." More specifically, the Stanford group, in examining three non-Western societies, focuses its attention on change, dynamic institutions, and notions of progress, which, according to Fields, points toward a Western orientation; with the use of examples, his explanation suggests implications that should demand the attention of all teachers of world history.

Finally in this section, in "Teaching World History," William H. McNeill calls upon his long experience as a teacher and historian of world history to present his thoughts on ways to approach the subject and on what has mattered most over time, including the human drive for power and wealth, along with the resulting changes, contacts with strangers, the open-endedness of human experiences, and the great variety of human norms and expectations. He then suggests ways to choose from "among the infinite possibilities that world history offers." Among other critical considerations are the process of innovation, the diffusion of skills, and the process of interaction across civilizations. He also cautions us not to ignore the costs as we survey the gains of human history.

The concluding section, *Regions and Civilizations,* is devoted to articles that, for the most part, highlight the major themes, concerns, and resources that are most useful for assisting nonspecialists in their world history courses when teaching about regions, areas, countries, and civilizations outside of Europe. In "Remapping the West: Teaching the Middle East in World and Western Civilization Courses," Joel Beinin emphasizes the many links between Middle Eastern and Western civilizations and traditions, along with the prevalence of Islam in the evolution of Afro-Eurasian societies. He suggests themes and sources from the history of the Middle East that can and should be incorporated into teaching world history survey courses, beginning with the origins of Western and Judeo-Christian civilization and continuing to the mediating role played by Islamic societies between the Hellenic tradition and Western Europe and between East Asia and the

Mediterranean region. All this should enable us to help our students to understand Arab and Islamic cultures as something other than hostile or foreign to Western traditions.

Colin A. Palmer, in "Distant Neighbors: Teaching About the Caribbean," calls our attention to the diverse societies that make up this region. Too often forgotten—and stereotypically portrayed when remembered—our neighbors to the south and southeast have played an important role in world history, both before and after 1492. What those roles have been, and are, and how they can be better understood, along with the themes worthy of attention and suggested readings, make up most of this selection.

Then William F. Sater reminds us of the great variety of people, cultures, and languages subsumed under the name Latin America so as to render it a misnomer. This, as he explains in "Joining the Mainstream: Integrating Latin America into the Teaching of World History," creates virtually insurmountable difficulties for efforts to include all of Latin America in a world history course. Instead, he advises dividing the continent into four racial/national blocs (Indian, mestizo, black/mulatto, white) as a means to acknowledge Latin America's diverse population while also making it manageable to incorporate into world history courses. He then proceeds to discuss the main themes of the region's history, starting with the eve of European intrusions around the time of Columbus, as well as comparative strategies teachers might implement; and he recommends a rich variety of sources that can be used to help bring teachers up to speed.

As a kind of an appendix to Sater, in "Making Latin American History Part of the Curriculum," Susan Shapiro recalls a brief story about a Latino student and her own lack of knowledge about his historical background to argue in favor of learning more about Latin American history and integrating it into the world history curriculum.

Next, in "Teaching India in a World History Survey," Tara Sethia directs our attention to the subcontinent of India and its myriad contributions "in defining the human heritage," both in Asia and beyond. In fact, Indian religion, inventions, innovations, and raw materials have all been integral to the development of world history. A fascination with teaching Indian history is often accompanied by frustrations (that is, "the connections between the images and the realities that have characterized Indian society"), both of which are addressed as Sethia suggests workable and reasonable approaches to making India one with world history courses. Among other things, she addresses the issue of how much time should be devoted to India, the topics that are likely to be most useful to include (and at what depth), and the difficulty in communicating concepts that are alien to most students. A select number of suggested readings are also provided.

Lastly, Peter N. Stearns writes about the United States, a country that is usually alien to world history courses and is often studied as if it were apart from the rest of the globe. As he explains in "Teaching the United States in World History," both world history and even the typical Western Civ survey are taught with only scattered attention paid to American history, just as histories of the United States pay only scant attention to the rest of the world. Stearns attempts to prod us toward rethinking this aspect of teaching both world and American history. He suggests several themes worthy of classroom exploration to achieve this integration, and he offers valid, if debatable, reasons for doing so. Since the history of the world has never been a simple bifurcated Us/U.S. and Them, neither should the history of the world we teach. There is also a lot here that will encourage lively discussion (for example, American exceptionalism, the United States as an extension of Western civilization, the perennial contradictions between American ideals and the history of slavery and discrimination). In short, and in the words of Tom Davis, Stearns shows us anew that—and why—"the world is round."

Robert Blackey
California State University, San Bernardino
April 1999

World History or Western Civilization?

Starting from Scratch: Shifting from Western Civ to World History

Thomas W. Davis ◆ December 1996

Since this article first appeared, the interest among college faculty in teaching world history courses has continued to grow. This interest has been manifested in many ways, for example, the rising membership in the World History Association and its regional affiliates, the growing number of world history sessions at professional meetings, the proliferation of world history textbooks now available from most major publishers, and the attention given the world history center developed at Boston's Northeastern University. Furthermore, the College Board and Educational Testing Service have recently announced their approval of an Advanced Placement world history course, with a national test for enrolled high school students, that will lead to college credits being awarded. Several publications, in addition to this one by the AHA, are particularly helpful to newcomers and practitioners in the field, among them Heidi Roupp, ed., Teaching World History, *and Ross E. Dunn, ed.,* The World History Teacher: Essential Writings in a Growing Field.*

Interest in this subject continues to focus primarily on the "how" to teach world history, far less on the "why." Lively debates concentrate on where to start such courses (chronologically) and what to cover. Many faculty see the virtues of team-teaching such a course, especially when it is first offered, and readily appreciate the advantages of collaboration on such matters as a common syllabus. Such cooperative ventures also include greater contact between high school and college faculty, who find they have much to share in the area of "what works" in teaching world history. There's an excitement and energy in the field of world history, and the subject seems here to stay.

◆　◆　◆　◆

I write this essay with all the zeal of a recent convert to world history who has been academically energized by his newfound devotion to the subject. I also write with at least some awareness of the problems involved in teaching the subject.

I began my career in 1972 as a specialist in British history. I happily taught the required two-semester Western civilization course for nearly twenty years. Having secured promotion and tenure, I could have continued with Western Civ until retirement. But something kept troubling me about the course. In particular, I wondered occasionally if the rumblings about world history within the profession were worth further consideration. Increasingly, the answer for me became a resounding "yes," not because of demands for multiculturalism, political correctness, a desire to attack Western Civ, or the ethnic diversity in my classrooms, but simply because of what I considered to be more "e.c."—educationally correct. It came down to a question J. H. Hexter once posed: Which of the two courses is more beneficial for our students? I like the way he phrased that question, because it can be used to validate both Western Civ and world history. But for today's students, who will be spending most of their adult lives in the twenty-first century, I came increasingly to see the advantages of world history.

Furthering my interest was a six-month faculty exchange in 1988 with Carl Smith, a noted Middle East scholar from San Diego State University. Teaching in southern California left me with several observations: (1) the American Civil War was not the staple in the curriculum; this was especially noteworthy to me as a Virginian; (2) the term "Pacific Rim" took on new meaning in San Diego; and (3) provincialism exists but with a different geographical perspective on the West Coast. I reflected on this point after one student remarked, "I'm working 'back East' next summer; I'm going to Arizona." But above all, I remember having an office near Carl's colleague, Ross Dunn, who more than anyone conveyed to me the satisfaction that comes from teaching world history. After six months, I returned to Virginia with a determination to leap into the world history arena. It took five years to develop a world history course at the Virginia Military Institute. I made the following discoveries along the way.

INSTITUTIONAL SUPPORT
Moving to world history becomes easier if you have the support and encouragement of your department head, academic dean, and college

president. I was fortunate to have all three on my side. My experience has been that deans and presidents are often supportive of academic innovations that respond to perceived needs in higher education. In Virginia, for instance, the state has made a major commitment to implement the recommendations of an influential report issued by the Commission on the University of the Twenty-first Century. One recommendation was to internationalize the curriculum to expose students to global perspectives. This shift in focus can be accomplished in many academic disciplines, but the obvious place to start for many educational leaders is with the introductory history course. Educational leaders like signs of innovation and fresh thinking in the curriculum. That does not automatically make them cheerleaders for world history, but the fact remains that the shift to global history is often seen by administrators as one positive way of responding to the educational needs of today and tomorrow. These leaders also favor innovations that do not require substantial changes in faculty staffing. I also find that boards of trustees are inclined to support the shift to global history, particularly those trustees who work in the business community and regularly think about international markets and the movement of goods and services across cultural boundaries.

DEPARTMENTAL SUPPORT

In a department that has long offered Western Civ as its basic first-year course, the idea of a transition to world history was not embraced uniformly by all the faculty with joy and eagerness. My colleagues' reactions ranged from healthy skepticism to guarded enthusiasm. I treated all responses with respect, including the view that Western Civ was the educationally preferable approach to introductory history.

A few of my colleagues expressed doubts along these lines: "My two-semester Western Civ course is already superficial, so how could I ever be satisfied if I had the entire globe to cover?" I replied by raising the issue of what we include and exclude in every course we teach, regardless of its scope. A specialist could easily conclude that a year-long course in the American Civil War is superficial because of all that's left out. As historians, we always face issues of selection and organization, whether the scope is local or global.

Another major argument was expressed this way: "As a twenty-year teacher of Western Civ, how could I ever teach myself enough about China, India, and Africa to feel comfortable—in a sense, legitimate—in front of a class?" This is a valid concern, but there is an appropriate answer. It boils down to personal professional commitment and the willingness to make time to read more broadly. Those who conclude that world history is the better course educationally will find or make the time to prepare, especially if there is institutional support. And teachers who

3

agree to teach world history *will* need help along the way, but I'll always remember this comment heard during my own transition: "Moving to world history will inevitably involve a lot of time devoted to reading and teaching yourself." For those who remain reluctant and daunted by the task of going global, another observation comes to mind: "Teaching world history is a lot easier than contemplating the task." In other words, "just doing it" is the way to overcome many of the anticipated problems.

TIME AND MONEY

There are many helpful people and useful resources available to faculty who want to begin teaching world history, but the journey will be immeasurably more difficult without two key ingredients. To start, colleges might consider small summer stipends to support the initial reading required to begin such a course. In addition, they might provide instructors with a reduced teaching load during the first year of offering the course. Because so many educational voices speak in favor of global awareness, institutions need to show their support in substantial ways.

In the fall semester of 1991, I took a sabbatical leave for the sole purpose of examining world history as an introductory course and making specific recommendations. I methodically worked my way through numerous books and articles, starting with selected issues of *The History Teacher* and with J. W. Konvitz's splendid collection of edited essays, *What Americans Should Know: Western Civilization or World History?*.[1] I obtained Kevin Reilly's useful *World History: Selected Course Outlines and Reading Lists from American Colleges and Universities,* and I reviewed readings suggested by Ross Dunn (for example, Douglas D. Adler and William F. Lye, "Dare We Teach World History? Dare We Not?" *The History Teacher* 20 [May 1987]: 327–32; Edward L. Farmer, "Civilization as a Unit of World History," *The History Teacher* 18 [May 1985]: 345–63; L. S. Stavrianos, "The Teaching of World History," *Journal of Modern History* 31:2 [June 1959]: 110–17; and H. Loring White, "A Technological Model of Global History," *The History Teacher* 20 [August 1987]: 497–517).[2] I also invited Michael Galgano of James Madison University and Carl Smith to share their world history experiences with my departmental colleagues in afternoon seminars. Teachers at James Madison University made the switch from Western Civ to world history several years ago, and I sought to benefit from their efforts.

A major boost came from my joining the World History Association and reading articles in the *Journal of World History* and the *World History Bulletin,* which are aimed at teachers wanting to get started in global history. I found the following articles from the *Journal* especially helpful: George E. Brooks, "An Undergraduate World History Curriculum for the Twenty-First Century," 2:1 (spring 1991): 65–79; J. R. McNeill, "Of Rats and Men: A Synoptic Environmental History of the Island Pacific,"

5:2 (fall 1994): 299–349; and Lynda Shaffer, "Southernization," 5:1 (spring 1994): 1–21. From the *Bulletin,* I benefited from Julia Clancy-Smith, "The Middle East in World History," 9:2 (fall/winter 1992–93): 30–4; Craig A. Lockard, "Integrating African History into the World History Course: Some Transgressional Patterns," 10:2 (fall/winter 1993–94): 21–31; and Loyd S. Swenson, "A Jump-Start Reading List for Prospective World History Teachers," 9:1 (spring/summer 1992): 26.

I savored the writings of William McNeill and Peter Stearns on world history, and I believe that despite their differences (for example, on the relative significance of cultural diffusion), the two share some thoughts in common. For instance, both contend that the study of global history prepares one for an understanding of the modern world—more so than any other introductory first-year history course. Both argue in favor of focusing initially on the major, enduring civilizations in the world and on their legacies, although McNeill stresses the contact between the regions as the primary motor that drives civilizations forward, while Stearns focuses more on the distinctive elements in different societies and on the forces that shaped their experiences. (See William McNeill, *Mythistory;* Peter Stearns et al., *World Civilizations: The Global Experience.*)

In addition to reading, I attended my first world history conference where I learned about the effectiveness of bringing area specialists to one's college for weeklong summer seminars—for example, engaging African or Middle Eastern experts to discuss the best books, themes, and organizing principles for teaching their subjects. I also learned from the conference where funding might be obtained for such seminars. Not incidentally, I was reminded that teaching universal history was once the norm and that the traditional Western Civ course had a definite history of its own, rising to prominence in this country only after World War I. (See Gilbert Allardyce, "The Rise and Fall of the Western Civilization Course," *American Historical Review* 87 [June 1982]: 695–743.)

When I completed my sabbatical, I wrote a report to the administration that outlined my conclusion: VMI should initiate a two-semester world history course for first-year students as a pilot project. In the three semesters that followed, I hammered out the details of the proposed course with my colleagues, who became increasingly supportive, especially when they saw I was not trying to draft any of them as reluctant participants. Further assistance came from my department chair, Blair Turner, a Latin American historian who had taught Western Civ for years; he proved quite eager to teach the new course. In the spring of 1993, Turner and I made final plans and selected books. For the first semester (pre-1500), we chose William McNeill's *History of the Human Community,* 4th ed., Peter Stearns's *Documents in World History,* and Ross Dunn's *Adventures of Ibn Battuta.* We began the course in fall 1993, and here's how we did it.

THE FIRST SEMESTER

The university registrar selected 100 first-year students from the entering class of 360 and placed them in world history; the remaining students were enrolled in Western Civ. We met with our world history students three times per week, with each week in the semester being devoted to one of McNeill's fourteen chapters. His chronological organization and emphasis on cultural diffusion provided the structure to our course and the framework for our lectures and discussions.

For the first meeting of each week, a lecture was presented to all the students. With fourteen major lectures in the course, Turner and I gave half of them, spread throughout the semester. The other seven were given by teachers in our community invited to discuss a particular aspect of each week's chapter in McNeill. For instance, a Far Eastern historian gave an overview of classical China (comparing the Yellow River communities in the north with those along the Yangtze to the south), the early Chinese dynasties, and the different philosophies espoused by the Legalists, Taoists, and Confucians. A Middle Eastern historian gave a lecture on Mohammed and the origins of Islam. Another colleague intrigued me with his talk on Africa before European contacts. I learned about Monomotapas and the city of Great Zimbabwe, and I also gained much from the lecturer who described the Mongols and their expansion over the steppes of Eurasia. During the past decade, my own department has hired several new teachers with area specialties beyond Europe and North America, a fact that helped us compose the lecture list.

In regard to my own lectures, I enjoyed researching and delivering a talk on early India and the Hindu religion and on the Kushite civilization in northeast Africa, but I think my favorite discovery was preparing a lecture entitled "The World in the Year One." I started my preparation by asking our reference librarian about calendars and differing methods of measuring time, learning for the first time what "the year one" was for the Chinese, the Jews, the Indians, and the Zoroastrians.

For the second meeting in the week, students attended one of eight discussion sections scheduled over a four-day period. Turner and I had about twelve students in each discussion group, and we expected them to be conversant each time we met on the content of the week's lecture and on the assigned chapter in McNeill's text. In our effort to improve the discussions, we emphasized techniques of good note taking, and we allowed students to consult their notes during the brief weekly quizzes that took place during our second weekly meeting. The quizzes were based solely on that week's lecture and textbook assignment.

After all the discussion sections had met, Turner and I were ready for the week's third session with our students, when we met collectively with our respective discussion sections (his three, my five) to review and expand upon the primary lessons of the week's material and to preview the coming week. We also used these meetings for periodic hour tests.

As for grades, we offered the students varied opportunities. In addition to weekly quizzes, two hour-long tests, and an examination that counted 30 percent of the final grade, we assigned two papers to be composed outside of class. The first was an essay addressing the question of why democracy developed in Greece but not in India and why the caste system emerged in India but not in Greece. The second paper required students to write an analytical review of Dunn's book. While some students complained about the difficulty of following Battuta's travels in unfamiliar parts of the world, most seemed willing to meet the cultural challenges posed by a book set in the fourteenth-century Islamic world; they also began to see the global interconnections in the Dar al-Islam. To assist students, I showed them the December 1991 issue of *National Geographic*, which featured a cover picture and major article about a modern-day replication of Battuta's journey. Somehow, reading that article and viewing a current picture of Adam's Peak in Sri Lanka seemed to help students. The proof of this book's educational usefulness came from the quality of papers students submitted. Perhaps my enthusiasm for Dunn's book and Battuta's travels also affected my students' willingness to engage this new material.

THE SECOND SEMESTER

For the second semester, Turner and I continued with McNeill's textbook (volume two, post-1500). We used Alfred Crosby's *Columbian Exchange* and Chinua Achebe's *Things Fall Apart* for outside reading and reports, plus one book on an aspect of world history that students selected themselves. Crosby and Achebe seemed particularly effective for teaching about the consequences of "culture contact" and for altering student perspectives.

CONCLUSIONS

In looking back at our initial foray into world history, Turner and I are pleased. Students accepted the course and its broad, global perspective more readily than we had expected. The final grades resembled the distribution in Western Civ. And the two teachers were happy to have had their own intellectual batteries recharged. While favoring the format just described, we recognize that other approaches could also work (for example, the traditional arrangement of a teacher meeting the same group of twenty-five or thirty students three times per week). Pedagogically, however, we benefited from our team approach featuring the common lecture at the beginning of each week, the common syllabus, and our working together to produce the course's common assignments and final examination.

We recognized after our first attempt at teaching the course that some areas were in need of improvement. For example, we now try to help our first-year students glean more from the weekly lectures by giving them samples of our own lecture notes and by asking all lecturers to distribute a topical outline at the start of their talks; this latter technique increases the attention level of our students as the fifty-minute lectures progress. In discussion classes, we strive to elicit more comments from the group and to have students respond to each other instead of engaging in two-way discussions with the teacher. We are seeking innovative techniques for teaching and learning more about geography, especially techniques and computer programs that take advantage of new technology in the classroom.

Although the "work-in-progress" sign is still hanging on our world history course, we are encouraged by the initial results and by a recent unanimous department vote to abandon the Western Civ course for world history. Teachers new to the subject are getting institutional support to assist their transition. As more colleagues consider making the transition from Western Civ to world history, more seem willing to "work up" a fresh lecture in a new field—as long as they can commit the time and complete the suggested readings. Visits from outside experts and discussions with more experienced world history teachers are helping novice instructors gain the confidence to "take over" new subject material.

For myself, I savor two comments made by students who were asked if the course had made any difference to them. One said: "I saw the movie *Malcolm X* during the holidays and understood the parts about Islam because I'd had your course." Another remarked: "I was at home with my girlfriend during vacation, watching *Jeopardy* on television. When the category of 'world religions' came up, I just devastated her with my answers; she couldn't believe all I knew." Another student told me that he understands China far better now, having read *The Analects* by Confucius; yet others tell me that they can read the morning newspaper with far more understanding, thanks to the course. I will gladly add those comments to my list of justifications for world history, a list headed by my favorite reason: the world is round.

SOURCES
1. Some of the helpful articles in *The History Teacher* include William McNeill, "Beyond Western Civilization: Rebuilding the Survey," 10 (August 1977): 509–48; Peter Stearns, "Periodization in World History Teaching: Identifying the Big Changes," 20 (August 1987): 561–80; Craig Lockard, "Global History, Modernization, and the World-System Approach: A Critique," 14 (August 1981): 489–515; and Julio C. Pino, "Notes on Teaching Comparative Modern Latin American History," 27 (November 1993): 73–8.

2. For teachers thinking about starting a world history course, I recommend the following books as good general studies: John Fairbank, Edwin Reischauer, and Albert Craig, *East Asia: Tradition and Transformation,* rev. ed. (Boston: Houghton Mifflin, 1989); Stanley Wolpert, *A New History of India,* 5th ed. (Oxford: Oxford Univ. Press, 1997): E. Bradford Burns, *Latin America: A Concise Interpretive History,* 6th ed. (Saddle River, N.J.: Prentice-Hall, 1993); Albert Hourani, *A History of the Arab People* (Cambridge, Mass.: Harvard Univ. Press, 1991); and Basil Davidson, *Modern Africa,* 2nd ed. (New York: Longman, 1989).

"Hisperanto": Western Civilization in the Global Curriculum

Michael F. Doyle ◆ May 1998

Editor's Note: This article originally appeared in the *ECCSSA Journal* (12:1, winter 1997, 42–50), the publication of the Eastern Community College Social Science Association. We reprint it here with the permission of the journal.

◆ ◆ ◆ ◆

The intention of this article was to encourage discussion on a controversial topic, and to that end, I judge it successful; the thoughtful response by Ross Dunn and Edmund Burke III printed in Perspectives *(October 1998) being one such example. However, I maintain that an entity traditionally identified as "Western Civilization" does exist and warrants continued and critical study. I further maintain that this is achieved most efficiently for our students in the modern, and evolving, Western Civilization survey. I wish to thank Lynn Hunt (Univ. of Pennsylvania) and William G. Shade and Mike Baylor (Lehigh Univ.) for reading drafts of the article and for encouraging me.*

◆ ◆ ◆ ◆

"What has Athens to do with Jerusalem?" asked the Christian apologist Tertullian in the second century, thereby implying that the Greek heritage had become irrelevant in the new dispensation. What possible utility could a knowledge of antiquity have to anyone in the new age? Something ominously akin to that seems to be at work in the effort to dilute, if not replace, the study of Western civilization in undergraduate education. One author has recently recounted the "Rise and Fall of the Western Civilization" course.[1] Others have referred, not exactly with the nostalgia of John Donne regarding those "bare ruined choirs," to the "last Eurocentric generation."[2] To support the continuation of Western Civ runs the risk of appearing reactionary or, worse yet, ethnocentric in this global age of inclusion.

When Clinton Rossiter wrote his *Conservatism in America,* he subtitled his text *The Thankless Persuasion.*[3] He did so because the liberal consensus seemed to be pretty much in place and accepted as a fait accompli. A similar sentiment surrounds "multiculturalism" and with it, world history. To challenge its place in the changing curriculum seems equally thankless. Not long ago, Donald Kagan, then dean of the college at Yale, told the incoming first-year students there that the study of Western civilization would be an integral part of their education. His penalty for speaking his mind was considerably less severe than that meted out to John Hus in 1415, but it nonetheless chills. Some students "hooted" him down and denounced him as a racist. In reporting the incident, the *Yale Daily News* identified Kagan as a "white male professor" who had apparently sent "what could be perceived as a dangerous message to this community."[4]

To speak of curricular issues is to step into a terrain booby-trapped with intellectual landmines. What motivates my presentation is simply this: What is best for our students? In my particular institution, a community college in New Jersey, students arrive with only a minimum exposure to the history of Western civilization, since it is not a high school requirement. Is it best for these students to gloss the history of the world in preference to learning about the very culture to which they belong?

Several reasons are adduced for replacing Western Civ, and most of them warrant serious consideration. Students sometimes do feel unconnected to the European past; the United States is increasingly non-European ethnically; and the course itself has, at least in the past, been used to celebrate the superiority of the West and to neglect all "others." Admittedly, textbooks as well as teachers not so long ago dealt with non-European or non-American peoples only as they related to the Europeans themselves, and then normally in a cavalier and condescending fashion.

Recently, authors of textbooks, informed by research in social and cultural history, have attempted to correct such deficiencies and have responded to the valid charges that the survey of Western Civ has traditionally neglected an awful lot of people and ideas. Presently, most Western Civ textbooks are no longer guilty of such egregious errors, in part because writing a text has indeed become a "hazardous" undertaking.[5] Many in fact have used the course to swing the pendulum in a corrective fashion sometimes to the other extreme. Most, however, treat the West in its totality, revealing its many warts and scars. The days have long passed when Western Civ had as its aim "to trace the roots of American liberty and democracy back along a particular track, the railhead usually being Hammurabi,...which exposes the fundamental ideological nature of the course."[6] Once upon a time, that characterization would have been quite accurate, but that no longer reflects the reality of Western Civ texts or its teachers. This has been accomplished by the thoughtful and persistent insistence of some that women, minorities, and "people without history" be incorporated into the coverage. One must strenuously challenge, for example, Peter Stearns's contention that contemporary texts celebrate Athens with only "passing reference" to its slavery.[7] The more popular texts in American undergraduate education expend a great deal of energy criticizing the "democracy" of Athens as well as the "new imperialism" of late nineteenth-century Europe. A perusal of some of the more popular college texts can easily document that claim. For instance, one respected text reminds readers that slavery was in fact "commonplace" in ancient Greece, and compares it to Mesopotamian slavery. The index makes further reference in nine separate lines to the institution of slavery in Western civilization.[8]

In his textbook, Mark Kishlansky informs the student that in classical Athens, "over one-quarter of the total population were slaves" and judges it "fundamental" to Athenian culture. He includes ten additional references to that institution in his index.[9]

Lynn Hunt, in her recent contribution to the field, counts twelve general entries under slavery in the index. More to the point, she discusses at length the significance of slavery in ancient Greece, where slaves worked, tutored, and might be killed "with impunity" by their owners. She concludes that the slaves of ancient Greece certainly contributed to the economy of Greek society but received little benefit or recompense for their efforts.[10]

Likewise, the discussion of women in all of the above texts is made central and not peripheral to Western civilization. The charge of Stearns simply has no merit any longer, and an examination of the texts refutes his contention.

Thanks to the prompting of world history representatives, many textbooks now also include (and not merely as a "caboose") the important contributions made by non-Western civilizations to the development of Western civilization from its very foundations in Mesopotamia and the Mediterranean basin. In that sense, the old Western Civ course has indeed "fallen."

I should note at the outset that the proponents of world history with whom I have had the good fortune to communicate have had a profound impact on my own thinking. In fact, much of my initial hostility to world history has been dissipated; I have revised, and continue to do so, my own thinking on the subject. Judging by the feedback on the Internet to the "thread" of Western Civ or world history discussion, the issue is by no means a settled matter among my colleagues on campuses throughout the United States. I am grateful especially to Ross Dunn and Sara Tucker for their informed and judicious responses to my queries. In addition, textbook authors such as Lynn Hunt, Mark Kishlansky, and John McKay have also provided me with some useful insights into the question. After my introduction to the Internet, I discovered that this very question had been discussed in some detail in 1994. And it continues to generate much debate, which testifies to a certain vigor in our profession.

Two incidents prompted my initial interest in this question (as well as my hostility). First, our dean asked me if I thought we ought to replace our tired old Western Civ course with a more "current" offering in world history. At the time, I paid little attention (she is not a historian, I thought), merely reporting the conversation to my colleagues who, like myself, expressed concern that such a strategy would further dilute what we already believed too thin. Later, the dean of instruction likewise indicated his belief that our department ought to be more inclusive and scuttle our Western Civ course. Again, he is not a historian. I did recall reading some articles in *Perspectives* that posited the end of the European focus in history, but again I paid little attention.[11]

Some time later, I received a notice about an upcoming meeting of the mid-Atlantic branch of the World History Association. I scanned the topics and areas to be discussed and saw nothing that hinted at dissent from the idea that world history had replaced Western Civ. I received encouragement to submit a proposal that would consider the validity and advisability of so doing. Amid some protests that my doubts had already been settled and hardly warranted attention, my proposal was accepted. I proceeded to ask my former graduate school professors if indeed world history had replaced Western Civ. They were taken aback by the suggestion and offered further encouragement along with my colleagues at Ocean County College to pursue this issue.

Discovering that our students are woefully ignorant of all history, I looked at what kinds of history high school students in New Jersey studied. Most take two years of American history and one year of world history. Not surprisingly, their lack of knowledge of European history borders on the scandalous. Professor Evelyn Edson of Piedmont Virginia Community College relates a tale not atypical of today's student when she recounts a student's question, "Wouldn't Socrates have died before he was born, if he lived from 469 to 399?"[12]

Next, I investigated what colleges, especially two-year schools, are offering as history courses. Among the nineteen community colleges in New Jersey, eleven offer Western Civ; three offer both surveys; and four offer only world history. Among New Jersey four-year institutions, Trenton State and Rutgers offer world history while Stockton, St. Peter's, Seton Hall, and Georgian Court stick with Western Civ. Obviously, there is no unanimity concerning which survey best suits the needs of students. Despite the fact that Western Civ remains the overwhelming preference among most colleges and universities (and also despite my misgivings), I do imagine that world history may eventually replace Western Civ as the choice of many if not most colleges and universities in the United States.[13] The appeal of "global" seems too popular in the present environment to avoid this. Certainly the ever-growing movement toward a "global marketplace" strongly encourages a global preparation for the work force. However, I hope that the history of Western civilization will continue to receive the treatment that it merits. I will outline in more detail how best to accomplish and ensure that.

My objections to world history fall into two distinct categories. World history advocates have addressed them, but not satisfactorily. The issues involve logistical and philosophical problems that seem presently to be somewhat insoluble though I remain hopeful that a solution will evolve. I should reiterate that the single most important question that I keep asking myself as a professional educator is, what is best for our students? I think that transcends any philosophical or historiographical concerns we might have.

First, the logistical problem of attempting to "cover it all." Naturally, no one, even in the more limited U.S. survey, manages to do so and we probably should stop trying. To try to do so can only lead to "virtual" history. If we attempted to teach Spanish and Russian and Korean in the same language class we would only confuse the student. Some would construct an entirely artificial language like Esperanto to accomplish that "global" feel. The danger of so much coverage is that we might well hurry our students through the world like Carmen Sandiego and leave them stranded.

A survey of some of the world history texts documents this point. Students assigned *Heritage of World Civilizations* leave Europe at the end of the Roman Empire and proceed to India, Iran, Africa, China, Japan, then Iran and India again before taking up the narrative with the Franks almost 200 pages later.[14] The McKay text sticks closer to the narrative.[15] It does so by assigning twenty-two pages to cover over eleven hundred years of African history. The next thirty pages manage to cover India, China, and Japan during a period of over a thousand years! Those pages simply will not do justice to the subjects. In fact, they do the subject a disservice. The interesting thing about the McKay text is that the volume on Western history lists the same authors as the one on world societies. Surprisingly, both texts are similar in length. In fact, the world history survey is 10 percent shorter![16] To accomplish this, some items included in the Western Civ text had to be excised, including health and medical issues in Frankish times, medieval town life, the Dominicans, and other topics.

One of the strategies employed is reduction in the coverage of Western history. One of the leading proponents of the world history movement and a recent convert to the cause, Peter Stearns, recommends a strategy of trimming, sometimes "radical" or "severe pruning."[17] Even the Renaissance lay victim to this Occam's razor, though I suspect he made that cut in jest.[18] Obviously, we all make decisions as to what to include and exclude in our surveys, which are, after all, just that. Only the publishing industry seems comfortable with this arrangement. They always miraculously manage to piece together a world history or Western Civ or American history course textbook that is fifteen chapters long; one for each week in the semester.

Some world history strategists (and realistic Western Civ teachers as well) acknowledge that covering it all is neither possible nor desirable. Therefore, the former elect to focus on "processes" or the "big events." Ross Dunn defines the latter as events big enough to have an impact on different cultures in a "shared experience."[19] Does that suggest that until an event becomes significant to a majority it lacks historical credibility? Originally, the scientific revolution had little impact beyond the couple of hundred individuals who even understood it. Yet, as one Western Civ text reminds us, this "quiet revolution" had "far-reaching implications."[20] A generation ago Herbert Butterfield argued that this revolution reduced historical movements like the Renaissance and the Reformation to the ranks of "mere episodes."[21] What of those male bastions of the medieval period—universities? Do they fail to warrant mention because of their obvious "minority" status that precluded them from being a "shared experience" for most?

Stearns argues that an "urgent need" to understand Africa and Asia exists.[22] There is no debate there, but would not a full course (taught by individuals with some expertise) better serve that need? In this, I would support Diane Ravitch who suggests a yearlong study of Western Civ and another year of non-Western civilizations.[23]

Another logistical problem is the issue of teacher preparedness. It seems that our students ought to be assured that their professor has some schooling in the areas being taught. Very few world historians, I suspect, have linguistic training in non-Western languages, which handicaps them significantly. I do not pretend to be informed and expert in all (not even most!) areas of European history, but my total lack of training in non-Western areas troubles me immensely. To "retool" seems to do a grave injustice to a field deserving of lengthy preparation. Many correspondents have indicated their willingness to undertake the challenge of so doing; but can one really keep current with developments in "world" history? (Again, I make no pretense of so doing even in my own area.) Perhaps this can be addressed by the graduate programs newly in place in institutions like the University of Hawaii, Rutgers University, and others. Specialization within the field of history (indeed within any area) does offer some virtues that have been part of the schooling of historians within the United States, and the training in world history seems to contravene that professional tradition.

Less troublesome than the simple logistics of offering world history in lieu of Western Civ and providing skilled professionals to teach it is the philosophical issue. Ross Dunn recounted a revealing incident that occurred innocuously enough while walking down the street in his own culturally and ethnically diverse neighborhood. He noticed a sea of faces, those of relative "newcomers" to America. On his way back home, he wondered if his own children would have the opportunity to learn about these immigrants and their personal reasons for leaving their natal homes and coming to California.[24] Perhaps he and I live in similar environments. Although quite sympathetic to Dunn's feelings about the wonderful opportunity to discover and understand other peoples, my own response to the incident differs (and I hope it will not be interpreted as mere ethnocentrism). I wondered if these latest groups of American immigrants would elect to learn about the culture and civilization they had chosen to live in. I also pondered what changes they might bring or attempt to effect in their new environment. I was also reminded that, for better or worse, the globe is becoming increasingly Western. How ironic to abandon the study of that civilization at what Francis Fukuyama calls, with some exaggeration, "the end of history." Still, the chief distinguishing characteristic of modernity is its "Westernness." It would seem that we ought to require our students to be conversant with the features of that civilization because of its very relevance rather than replacing it due to its perceived irrelevance!

Western Civ does, in fact, require our students to confront other cultures. A Western Civ text (and course) should present the features of that other civilization or culture, not just as they appeared to Western eyes, but on their own terms. Certainly Western Civ students should read parts of the Qur'an and understand the attitudes that produced Fanon's *The Wretched of the Earth*. Indeed, as Stearns has rightly argued, we have "to treat non-Westerners as players in their own right and not simply as recipients of Western impulses and guidance."[25] I think no Western Civ instructor could possibly dissent from such a praiseworthy goal.

Because of what Theodore Von Laue identified as the world revolution of Westernization, a Western Civ course (properly sculptured) offers the student the best background to understanding the forces presently dominating much of the world and making informed comparisons.[26] Harvard historian David Gordon argued similarly that a Western Civ course would expose the student to many "unsavory ideas" and force the student to confront important and continuing issues with a solid foundation.[27] Naturally there are only so many classes that we can require our undergraduate students to take. As historians, we would prefer to see the number of history courses increased. Given the limitations of the school year, we have to make decisions. World historians declare that their choice is the better because it connects people of the increasingly diverse population with the history they study. Others argue that our ignorance of non-Western societies will hamper us economically in the future in an increasingly complex global economy. Still others opine that without seeing the whole picture of human history we stay focused on the particular only, and consequently miss the larger landscape. All of these are excellent reasons for enlarging our vision in the survey course so that we survey not just the familiar but the "foreign" as well.

The question becomes which vehicle will best allow our students to accomplish these estimable goals. Western Civ proponents want to ensure that we study our own civilization and understand exactly how it came to be what it is. If, as some world history advocates suggest, we accord all civilizations equal time then, as William McNeill reminds us, none can be considered essential.[28]

In the existing Western Civ surveys, the students already have their hands full. To edit more from it and to add other civilizations in its place would cause us to lose the narrative and, consequently, the coherence of history. As Theodore Rabb of Princeton concluded, our first responsibility has to be teaching the fundamentals of Western Civ. Only then can the student branch out.[29] Peter Stearns's idea was to select certain themes or processes and limit them to three or four to enable the student to find patterns that allow generalizations to link all civilizations; this certainly makes the world history course "doable," but it fragments the past and risks losing the student in the process.[30]

Fritz Stern edited an instructive book a generation ago entitled *The Varieties of History* in which he offered several examples of how historians have defined their roles and philosophies of history. He was not troubled by the changing face of history. "Nothing is more characteristic of the history of the last 200 years than the demand from within the profession that history must once again become broader, more inclusive, more concerned with the deeper aspects of human experience."[31] At the close of the century, a similar demand is being heard. What historians have to decide is how best to serve the needs of the student and the integrity of history.

In order to keep the question alive, I would like to offer some alternatives to the either/or proposition of dropping Western Civ altogether or retaining it and dropping world history. Neither, it seems, will simply disappear. Lynne Cheney recommended that students take six credits of Western Civ and six more of non-Western history, along with three credits in American history.[32] As desirable as this scheme is, it is equally unrealistic. Students will simply not accept the burden of so many history requirements.

In light of that, one recommendation to replace the "Western Civ or world history" alternative is the following. Western Civ should be reconfigured into two distinct courses. The first would focus on the ancient world to the Renaissance or Reformation, which pretty much replicates the existing "Civ One" course. The second half of the course would focus on the interaction between the West and the world. It is during this course that time could be spent developing a world perspective that would not interrupt the narrative but would in fact complete it. In his classic, *The Rise and Fall of the Great Powers,* Paul Kennedy made no apology that the book had a "heavily Eurocentric" thrust. In fact, he judged it "only natural."[33] As Jacques Ellul observed, the entire world has become "heir to the West."[34]

William McNeill, whose important work *Rise of the West* basically established the world history movement, also focused on Europe's central role in the making of the modern world.[35] Yet even he did not attempt to include "everyone" in his survey. He defended the continuation of separate national histories to supply that natural need that everyone has for a sense of history.[36]

The above solution to the present "troubles" in the discipline is actually not my first choice. I would prefer to continue two courses in Western Civ and add a required course for all students on the history of the twentieth-century world along with an additional course in a non-Western field. The recent work of Eric Hobsbawm might serve as an organizational model for such a useful and "doable" course. Like most in the discipline, however, it is regrettably a text that could be read by only a minority of our students.[37] (I haven't even mentioned the role of reading level in the choice of texts as well as courses for our students, but it certainly is an issue of increasingly important consideration.)

The needs of our students are best met by teaching them first and foremost about their own civilization and all the contributions made by others to it; this instruction needs to be an informed one. We are too much in the habit, I suspect, of applying the cant of bumper stickers to our profession: think globally, act locally. If the world history survey attempts to cover the world in the same space in which we previously covered Western Civ, the attempt must surely fail. The narrative that most students (and readers) need is sacrificed and the student is offered a smorgasbord or sampler which, like a wallpaper book, would stupefy and confuse.

My final option would be: Allow the issue to be sealed in the marketplace. Colleges ought to work to offer both world history and Western Civ surveys so that educators provide the fullest spectrum of information to their students and allow each individual to determine the preferred route. My only entreaty is to focus the world option on a thorough treatment of the West as well as for Western Civ to continue to incorporate a more inclusive approach to all cultures with which it came into contact. The chief beneficiary of this would be the student, who lives in Western civilization, attends an institution founded in the West, and is presumably a part of that civilization.

NOTES

1. Gilbert Allardyce, "The Rise and Fall of the Western Civilization Course," *American Historical Review* 87 (1982): 695–743. More recently see Thomas Davis, "Starting from Scratch: Shifting from Western Civ to World History," *Perspectives* (December 1996): 1; reprinted in this volume.

2. John R. Gillis, quoting Caroline Walker Bynum in "The Future of European History," *Perspectives* (April 1996): 1.

3. Clinton Rossiter, *Conservatism in America: The Thankless Persuasion* (New York: Vintage Books, 1962).

4. Quoted in Richard Bernstein, *Dictatorship of Virtue: Multiculturalism and the Battle for America's Future* (New York: Alfred A. Knopf, 1994), 50.

5. Joyce Appleby et al., *Telling the Truth about History* (New York: Norton, 1994), 294.

6. Ross Dunn, e-mail to the author, August 7, 1996.

7. Peter Stearns, *Meaning over Memory: Recasting the Teaching of Culture and History* (Chapel Hill: University of North Carolina Press, 1993), 82.

8. John McKay et al., *A History of Western Society,* 5th ed., vol. 1 (Boston: Houghton Mifflin, 1995), 87–89.

9. Mark Kishlansky et al., *Civilization in the West,* 2nd ed., vol. 1 (New York: HarperCollins, 1995), 72–75.

10. Lynn Hunt et al., *The Challenge of the West,* vol. 1 (Lexington: D.C. Heath & Co., 1995), 57–8. See also Donald Kagan et al., *The Western Heritage,* 5th ed. (Englewood Cliffs, N.J.: Prentice Hall, 1995), 46, 88–90.

11. Gillis, 1.

12. Evelyn Edson, "The Historian at the Community College,"

Perspectives (October 1996): 17.

13. In addition, Mark Kishlansky of Harvard indicated that his Western Civ text outsold his world text by roughly three to one. Personal correspondence.

14. Albert Craig et al., *The Heritage of World Civilizations* (New York: Macmillan, 1994).

15. John McKay et al., *A History of World Societies,* vol. I (Boston: Houghton Mifflin, 1996).

16. As one of the authors happily reports in McKay, *World Societies,* preface, xix.

17. Stearns, 181–85.

18. Stearns, 188.

19. Ross Dunn, "Central Themes for World History," in Paul Gagnon et al., eds. *Historical Literacy: The Case for History in American Education* (New York: Macmillan, 1989), 220.

20. Hunt, 571.

21. Herbert Butterfield, *The Origins of Modern Science, 1300–1800,* rev. ed. (New York: The Free Press, 1965), 7.

22. Stearns, 8.

23. Quoted in Dunn, "Central Themes," 219.

24. Dunn, "Central Themes," 216–17.

25. Stearns, 46.

26. Subtitled *The Twentieth Century in Global Perspective* (New York: Oxford University Press, 1987).

27. "Inside the Stanford Mind," *Perspectives* (April 1992): 8.

28. William McNeill, "Pursuit of Power: Criteria of Global Relevance," in Gagnon, 107.

29. Theodore K. Rabb, "Old and New Patterns for the History of Western Civilization," in Gagnon, 214.

30. Stearns, 105.

31. Fritz Stern, ed. *The Varieties of History: From Voltaire to the Present* (Cleveland: World Publishing Co., 1956), 12.

32. Cited in Stearns, 80.

33. Paul Kennedy, *The Rise and Fall of the Great Powers: Economic Chance and Military Conflict from 1500 to 2000* (New York: Random House, 1987), xxi.

34. Jacques Ellul, *The Betrayal of the West* (New York: Seabury Press, 1978), 21.

35. William McNeill, *Rise of the West: A History of the Human Community* (Chicago: University of Chicago Press, 1963).

36. McNeill, "What Do We Teach," in Gagnon, 136.

37. Eric Hobsbawm, *The Age of Extremes: A History of the World, 1914–1991* (New York: Vintage Books, 1956).

Freedom in World History:
Can Parachutists and Truffle-Hunters
Find Happiness Together?

Alan T. Wood ◆ January 1991

I had two purposes in mind when I wrote this essay almost ten years ago. The first purpose was to propose the resurrection of human freedom as a suitable organizing principle in world history. Since then I have come to believe that freedom can best be understood in relation to authority, a theme I have explored in a book entitled What Does It Mean to be Human?: Balancing Freedom and Authority in World History. *The second purpose was to argue that world history ought to be an integral part of both the undergraduate and graduate curricula. I thought then, and still do, that the broad perspective afforded by the study of the human condition as a whole is complementary and not antithetical to the highly specialized research most of us engage in as professional historians. But world history is rarely taught at major research universities, and almost never at the graduate level. For K–12 teachers (and college professors) who are assigned world history courses without the benefit of any undergraduate or graduate preparation, as well as for students entering careers in global companies, our universities are not much help.*

I suspect we all understand the reasons for this state of affairs. Bureaucratic momentum keeps institutions grinding inexorably forward even when there is every reason to stop or head in a different direction. As an administrator I understand that imperative. Indeed, I am one of the chief grinders. Nevertheless, I cannot help wondering whether we have not become as complacent and unresponsive to change as British universities were at the end of the nineteenth century. Accustomed to giving their young people a general education suitable for leadership of an empire, Oxford and Cambridge professors were in the habit of turning up their noses at applied sciences like engineering. While they napped, their German counterparts pumped out tens of thousands of engineers, helping to catapult Germany into the status of a major world power. Have we not put ourselves equally out of touch with the world around us (albeit at the opposite extreme of exalting specialists and despising generalists)? In our enthusiasm over specialized research have we not forgotten that in the world of practical affairs everything is connected to everything else? To be sure, there has been progress in the past ten years. Unfortunately, it has been slow progress. Meanwhile yet another generation of students (and future teachers) has slipped through our fingers without adequate preparation for global citizenship.

◆　◆　◆　◆

L et me begin by giving an affirmative answer to the question posed in the title of this essay—parachutists and truffle-hunters can find perfect happiness together, although at the moment they are not talking to each other, at least not in a language the other can understand. Parachutists, of course, are generalists, who take a broad view of matters, and truffle-hunters are specialists, who have an accurate understanding of very specific subjects. Their marriage, a once-blissful union that gave birth to many of the great teachers and scholars of the past, is now on the rocks. Ever since modern colleges and universities chopped up knowledge into bite-size chunks known as departments, an academic aristocracy composed primarily of truffle-hunters has come to dominate higher education.

When H. G. Wells—an early parachutist—published his *Outline of History* in 1920, he complained that the study of history had become too partial and narrow, and the volume of specialized research too much for one mind to absorb. He could not have imagined then that the little mounds of monographs that dotted the academic landscape in his lifetime would grow by the end of the century to become vast and impassable mountain ranges, severing communication between the disciplines of knowledge (and even between the subdisciplines of history) and fostering the proliferation of mutually unintelligible dialects.

Faced with such daunting obstacles, the prospect of doing world history well, either in a classroom or between the covers of a book, would appear to be growing more remote with each passing year. On the other hand, as our knowledge continues to fracture, the need for such a unifying perspective may be even greater. The fact that our microscopes can now peer at smaller and smaller objects on an elephant's hide does not mean we can forget about the whole elephant. In the same vein, if a visitor to New York wants to find out how to get from Rockefeller Center to the New York Public Library, he looks at a map of New York, but if he wants to find out how to get from New York to Nairobi, he looks at a map of the world. One map is not better or worse than the other. They simply have different uses. In the modern research university, unfortunately, there is no academic equivalent of a map of the world.

Let me try to put my own views on world history in the larger context of the profession as a whole. We live in a world dominated by science. The purpose of science is to investigate the behavior of objects in the natural world to predict and ultimately to control that behavior for the benefit of society. During and after the Enlightenment it was hoped that the "scientific method" might also be used to understand and improve the behavior of human beings. The social sciences were born. To be sure, some Enlightenment thinkers got a little carried away when they anticipated that human nature could someday be perfected. But one does not have to believe in human perfectibility to hope that human suffering can be ameliorated through understanding more thoroughly the social and psychological forces that act upon us. To that noble purpose the social sciences committed their prodigious energies.

There is one area that science does not treat, however, and that is meaning. If a given scientist were to inquire into the meaning of gravity rather than its properties or effects, most of her colleagues would likely conclude she had gone a bit soft in the head. Meaning is taken to be a matter best left to philosophers whom nobody reads anyhow, at least in the United States (or so said de Tocqueville, and little has changed since).

The academic study of history has understandably reflected these scientific assumptions. In the United States, historical study came to be modeled on the nineteenth-century German institution of the graduate research seminar, which encouraged scholars to focus on very small subjects and to orient their research to the discovery of new knowledge. The final product of the scholarly enterprise became the monograph, dealing with a single subject limited in time and space. The bureaucratic imperatives of the modern academy further narrowed that scope. Among the least beneficial of those imperatives is a propensity to define success in terms of quantity rather than quality, the former being more readily accepted as equitable and fair than the latter, which is unquestionably messy and difficult to measure. Because one can produce quantity more quickly by focusing on narrow subjects, the pressure to do so is irresistible. Those who are best at it rise to the top, from which lofty heights they survey the wreckage, pronounce it wonderful, and do everything in their power to ensure that the system, which so wisely recognized their worth, is continued to the end of time. The result is that the modern university stresses analysis at the expense of synthesis. One of the rare occasions historians ever talk about synthesis is when they give the presidential address at the annual meeting of the AHA, after which the members of the audience, and the president, deploy back to their analytical foxholes. (I read through all the presidential addresses one summer a few years ago. I highly recommend the exercise. It is inspiring.)

The intellectual energy of the university is produced by fission, not fusion, and the forces released by that energy are centrifugal, not centripetal. Robert Hutchins was not far off when he described the modern university as a collection of separate departments unified by a central heating system.

In any case, the ultimate object of a social science is to discover underlying patterns and laws of human behavior. Most of the views of world history appearing in the twentieth century have had this same purpose: the organic metaphor of Spengler, the challenge/response paradigm of Toynbee, Marxism and its current permutation in the form of dependency theory, cultural diffusion, various forms of modernization theory, and applications of sociological or anthropological paradigms of one sort or another. I do not wish to deny the validity of any of these approaches. On the contrary, I have the highest regard for the insights they have given us. Coleridge is supposed to have remarked once that men are usually right in what they affirm and wrong in what they deny, and in that spirit let me stress that my primary criticism of professional monographs is not that they are narrow—they have to be—but that there is no place for anything other than the monograph. To put it another way, historians are right in affirming the value of analysis, and wrong in denying the value of synthesis. My quarrel with specialists is not that they are different from generalists, but that they shoot them on sight.

Intellectual breakthroughs, after all, are the product of the synthesizing impulse. The analytical process is best suited for verifying or refuting insights originally arrived at through the free play of the imagination. Insofar as our institutions of higher learning discourage synthesis they threaten to dry up the springs of intellectual life in this country or divert them into think tanks that tend to be driven more by ideology than a search for the truth. The old cliché that the world is divided into problems and universities are divided into departments (with very little connection between the two) may have some truth to it after all.

My own particular approach to synthesis on a grand scale does not pretend to have discovered a new pattern of human behavior, but is organized around a universal problem in the manner of a Greek play. The world history I have in mind is indebted to Greek tragedy, and to Thucydides. History is, among other things, a great drama, in which the human race is the protagonist. Endowed with prodigious gifts, this protagonist has free will, encounters forces over which he has no control, makes a serious error in judgment based upon a fundamental flaw in his own makeup, and then suffers far more than he deserves as a result. The suffering, as in *Oedipus Rex* (and *Oedipus at Colonus*), may be redemptive, but that does not wash away the simple fact that the innocent suffer along with the guilty. Thucydides carried out this basic plan, in which Athens—free and cosmopolitan, the fountain of democracy and philosophy—came to a grievous end because its citizens were corrupted by disease (over which they had no control) and power (over which they did have control) and brought about their own destruction as a result.

In Genesis, the temptation offered by the reptile in the Garden of Eden was for Adam and Eve to become like God by eating of the fruit of the tree of the knowledge of good and evil. As the inhabitants of paradise freely chose that fruit, so has the human race aspired to become like God through its mastery of the forces of nature, approaching ever closer to the divine prerogative both to create and destroy life.

My focus is on freedom, tracing the development of the human race in all its cultural variety from very early times to the present, showing how free will and human genius have combined to increase man's control over the forces of nature but always with the tragic imperative at work. That control, from the domestication of fire on to the harnessing of nuclear energy, is available for good and for evil, for ameliorating suffering and for magnifying it. The two go hand in glove.

Lord Acton, one of the most influential historians of the nineteenth century, was always on the point of beginning work on a universal history, which he never quite got around to. Toward the end of his life his friends took to referring to the project as the greatest book never written. Instead, Acton acted as editor of the *Cambridge Modern History*—not too shabby an accomplishment, to be sure, but a work of specialists nonetheless. Had he written his own world history, I suspect he would have organized it around freedom, which he virtually identified with progress and human perfectibility. We ought to pick up where Acton left off (although not necessarily with his faith in the malleability of human nature—the intervening century has, alas, rather tarnished that hope).

My approach is to divide the activities of the human race into six categories: politics, economy, society, philosophy/religion, aesthetics (art, literature), and science/technology. In each of these areas, it seems to me, the notion of freedom can act as a kind of clothesline on which to hang the otherwise diverse expressions of human genius. The economic problem, for example, is how to gain greater control over the productive forces (thereby expanding the range of choice), and distribute their fruits equitably.

The political realm is more obviously one of increasing or decreasing freedoms. Incidentally it is here that many of my own colleagues in non-Western studies have often criticized my clothesline, arguing that by focusing on freedom I am guilty of imposing my Western cultural assumptions on societies that do not have such values. I hope that the events in China in June 1989 put that argument to rest forever. One must make a clear distinction between the impulse to freedom, which I believe to be universal, and the existence or development of enabling institutions, which may vary a good deal from society to society and from time to time. That the Chinese have the desire, and not the enabling institutions, is now—courtesy of CNN—clear to all the world.

Freedom itself, of course, is not to be understood only in its negative form as an absence of restraint, but also in its positive form as the opportunity to bring to fruition something that had previously existed in a potential state. In this sense, the outward expression of man's creative genius in art and literature, the deepened understanding of meaning that developed as human religious and philosophical systems grew more complex, are all a part of this underlying impulse toward freedom.

What I offer is an organizing principle for the study of world history that is based upon a fundamental problem in the human condition rather than a search for a pattern or law of behavior. This is clearly an understanding of history that departs from the belief that history is primarily a science focusing on the advancement of knowledge. Insofar as my view emphasizes meaning as well as knowledge, I suppose that what I offer is closer to art than science, but I stress again that my approach is not intended to be a substitute for the conventional way of organizing history but a complement.

The great French historian and sociologist of Chinese religion Marcel Granet, who died shortly after the fall of France in 1940, is supposed to have declared to his class once (presumably *before* he died, though with some French intellectuals you can't be too sure): "I don't give a damn about China. What interests me is man." I suspect that if Granet were a recent PhD looking for a teaching job in the United States, with an attitude like that he would probably end up selling pencils on the street corner. If Granet meant what I think he meant, however, we could use a few more like him around now.

We know more about the world than we did, but we do not know the meaning of what we know, and it is that very meaning that is so urgently required. The problems brought about by rapid technological change, by the struggles between religions and between a multitude of ideological surrogates for religion, by overpopulation, by environmental pollution, and by proliferating nuclear weapons, far transcend in their destructive potential those that confronted individual civilizations in the past. In the face of these circumstances, historians—who have a special responsibility for educating the public in their civic responsibilities—should address themselves, however peripherally, to these urgent questions, with a view to forging out of the diverse national traditions of the world a greater sense of common purpose. Only when the world realizes the degree to which each civilization manifests qualities and experiences common to all civilizations, only when it understands the ways in which the different forms of civilized experience give expression to a common impulse to order and meaning in life, will we be in a position to confront our problems with a reasonable prospect of success. The perspective gained from a study of world history is vital to this enterprise. If such a pragmatic motive in the writing of history is criticized as imposing an unnatural burden of didactic morality on the interpretation of the facts then I can only respond that facts do not always speak for themselves. Perhaps more interpretation would shorten the unnecessarily large gap between a public desperately in need of wisdom, and the historian in need of a public. In the words of Louis Gottschalk (in another presidential address),

> let [the historian] also pray for the courage combined with the humility necessary to employ his historical training and insight as well as he can for the guidance of an unmoored society seeking firmer anchorage.[1]

We are all of us dependent, in one way or another, on the fortunes of the world around us. We must not allow that link, which binds the objects of our study to the need of the larger community for a clear statement of means and ends, to be permanently severed. Paul Gagnon makes a strong plea for just this kind of approach to the teaching of history:

> It takes a sense of the tragic and the comic to make a citizen of good judgment, as it does a bone-deep understanding of how hard it is to preserve civilization or to better human life, and of how it has nonetheless been done, more than once in the past. It takes a sense of paradox, not to be surprised when failure teaches us more than victory does, or when we slip from triumph to folly. And maybe most of all it takes a practiced eye for the beauty of work well done, in daily human acts of nurture."[2]

Here I seek only to remind the interested reader of the importance of a universal perspective in history, and to suggest that we should no more abandon the study of world history because of its inherent difficulties than we should cease trying to become better persons because we cannot become perfect. Recall for a moment Chesterton's marvelous remark (which should be carved in stone and hung around the necks of all academic perfectionists), that if something is worth doing, it is worth doing badly.

Most history departments in major research universities in the United States devote very little if any attention to the subject of world history. Faculty members whose prospects for tenure and promotion are related to the number of publications they produce in their field of expertise are naturally reluctant to pursue a subject that might slow down the progress of their own careers. Added to this is their understandable hesitation to indulge in generalizations about areas of the world that lie outside the scope of their own academic preparation, and that would expose them to professional criticism by specialists in those areas. These obstacles cannot be dismissed lightly, nor do I know of any easy way by which they might be removed, and yet they do not diminish our responsibility to broaden and deepen the nature of the questions we ask of the historical record. We now have within our grasp, because of the great contributions of the social sciences in the last two centuries in widening our knowledge of the past, the tools to undertake this great task. What we seem to lack is the vision and the will. We need, in short, more airborne truffle-hunters.

NOTES

1. *American Historical Review* 59 (January 1954): 286.

2. *Democracy's Half-Told Story: What American History Textbooks Should Add* (Washington, D.C.: American Federation of Teachers, 1989),157.

Perspectives on Teaching World History

A Declaration of Interdependence: World History for the Twenty-First Century

Theodore H. Von Laue ◆ April 1993

In the past six years my basic perspectives have not changed. The only addition I would have made, were I several decades younger with the capacity to explore a new and growing field, would have been to stress the importance of environmental history as an integral part of world history. My final reflections on world history, an expanded version of the ideas advanced here, were published under the title "World History, Cultural Relativism, and the Global Future," in World History: Ideologies, Structures, and Identities, *edited by Philip Pomper, Richard Elphink, and Richard T. Vann.*

◆ ◆ ◆ ◆

Teaching world history poses perhaps the biggest challenge for the present generation of academic historians. It therefore deserves continuous discussion. There is no dearth of available facts. What we need are proper perspectives and an enlarged vision for organizing these facts in order to gain a clearer understanding of where we *all* have come from and where we are headed, thus seeking to achieve better control over human destiny. As responsible teachers we must prepare our students for a difficult future in our ever more interdependent world by constant experimentation promoting constructive insights into the complexity of human affairs past and present.

This ambitious goal requires—to state the thrust of this essay at the outset—that we rise above the major division of opinion among world history teachers (and concerned intellectuals generally). In our interdependent world we need to be keenly aware of the contributions to human development made in the past by the people of Africa, Asia, and Latin America; we need to stress cultural diversity because we are a culturally diverse nation in a culturally diverse world. But approaching the twenty-first century, we must also face another reality: there is no escape from the intense interdependence based on Western achievements. In other words, we should combine a compassionate appreciation of cultural differences with a search for common values and practices that promote peaceful worldwide cooperation; cultural relativism must be absorbed into the absolutes of global unity pioneered by the West—a challenging but unavoidable professional task if we want to help create a more humane world. Stressing the Western-induced intense global interdependence of the present and the future is not prompted by a Eurocentric bias, but by a panhuman perspective.

I. Several major assumptions are implicit in this approach. First, the main purpose of world history is to help our students acquire a better grasp of the forces shaping our world both at present and in the foreseeable future. As Lord Acton observed, "We study history in order to overcome it." We need more insights into the dynamics of our times in order to counter the growing confusion over the purpose of life and to reduce the inhumanities so prominent in our world. The living, it is clear, have precedence over the dead; they have the right to examine the past in the light of their own search for a better future. Responsible world history, therefore, must begin with an effective grasp of the present in all its troubling aspects. In what kind of world do we live? What can we learn from the past in order to cope more effectively with the challenges of our times? A live and relevant history extends forever forward in time.

Next, we need to evolve meaningful generalizations rather than dote on detail. We must keep in mind the brevity of the academic year, as well as the overload of knowledge to be mastered and the undersupply of available human energy in our overstimulated society generally, and, as all teachers are aware, among our students particularly. Under these conditions we must concentrate on essentials so as to take young minds beyond memory lane. For instance, rather than list the names of kings or monarchs, we should describe the character and role of monarchy; rather than enumerate the peculiarities of a given religion, we should attempt a comparison with competing faiths that promotes understanding. In short, we must simplify the mind-boggling complexity of the past, devising syntheses and overviews, while also judiciously allocating the available time between past and present. In settled times, when people feel secure, there may be justification for mental immersion into the infinities of bygone days. But in the present worldwide insecurity where people worry about their future, the recent past and the present claim top priority. We therefore owe our students as accurate a grasp as possible of the world in which they are going to shape their lives. We must help them to overcome history, instead of being sucked back into it. A world history course certainly should not tempt us to bury our heads in the past.

The study of world history, furthermore, demands that we venture an all-inclusive cultural analysis of historical evolution. That is, in offering explanations for the diversity of historical development in various parts of the world, we must have an adequate understanding of *all* the factors at work, including geography (which incorporates climate and the environment), the most fundamental determinant of collective achievements and cultural interaction. In addition, we have to be aware of variations in moral values, patterns of thinking, approaches to science and technology, economic productivity, political organization, and—another key item—status in the world. All these factors combined add up to the driving force in human history: the cultural capacity to survive or to dominate, whether by the arts of war or of peace, or, most commonly, by a combination of both. Historical analysis and periodization, like contemporary civic attention, should be centered on the many-sided dynamics of political power, a factor unconsciously minimized by most American political scientists and historians. Are they willing, for instance, to admit how much the worldwide influence of the British empire and the United States has inspired Stalin, Hitler, Mao Zedong, and prominent dictators in Asia, Africa, and Latin America? Are we, as teachers, willing to help our students to understand the complex circumstances and resources that led the West (taken as a whole) to achieve a global ascendancy unprecedented in all history?

Next, we should always emphasize the power of envious comparison. As Thomas Hobbes observed several centuries ago, "Man, whose Joy consisteth in comparing himself with other men, can relish nothing but what is eminent." In the contemporary age, envy of what is eminent is a worldwide political force. Large numbers of non-Western people, exerting an elemental upward pressure toward personal wealth and power, want to live like Westerners (and, foremost, Americans). Dealing with this troublesome fact, our historical analysis should be all-inclusively comparative, matching the resources of one part of the world against others. Such comparison should be guided by the recognition that the differences in living standards and power, now so keenly deplored, have often been caused by circumstances beyond human control, by the very diversity of the world's surface. Life in the tropics at the edge of deserts cannot possibly match the resources of cool and fertile lands. The survival skills of sub-Saharan people, for instance, may be as subtly complex as those of Europeans, but not in terms of political power and economic productivity. The patent inequality among people around the world—so a world history course should emphasize—is in the last analysis the result not merely of human design or cunning, but of many circumstances beyond human control. It is a tragic reality built into the nature of Mother Earth, to be treated, like any tragedy, with a compassionate resolve to overcome the unfortunate consequences. And that tragedy must not be compounded by transforming environmental inequalities into human—ethnic or racial or cultural—inequalities as well.

For this reason we need to infuse into the teaching of world history an expanded sense of moral responsibility. We are tied to more than five billion other human beings in our interdependent multicultural world. The more intense the human contexts in which we operate, the more refined must be our moral sensibilities. Inevitably we touch highly sensitive moral nerves when we confront alien people and cultures; witness, for instance, the American gut reaction to the Tiananmen massacre in 1989. But in trying to devise a world history that does justice to human diversity, we must deal compassionately even with repulsive political regimes that have evolved in geographic and historic settings different from our own. We must try to understand them on their own ground, from within, not on Western (or distinctly American) terms, as is commonly done. All along, we need to be morally sensitive to the position of minorities, women, and children in the societies and cultures we discuss.

By the same logic, responsible world history demands that we transcend our conventional American morality, which has evolved under exceptionally favorable historical conditions. This is a profound challenge destined to provoke embittered controversy. Who, for example, would dare to view the shooting of the demonstrators on Tiananmen Square from Deng Xiaoping's perspective? But the logic of world history living up to its promise calls for understanding the motives on the other side. It combines the cultural relativism born of compassionate understanding across cultural and political boundaries with a transcendent sense of the common humanity that we want to promote as teachers of world history. Only if we accept other people as their own circumstances have shaped them can we proceed to establish the common ground required for peaceful cooperation.

Finally, our recognition of cultural pluralism must be combined with stressing the common skills and goals that guide the contemporary world and the future. Regardless of their indigenous roots, all people now depend on the human capacities needed for the successful management of our intensely competitive global interdependence for the common benefit. These skills and goals have reached their most sophisticated level yet in Western culture. They are based on a combination of widespread literacy, capacity for abstract thinking, a puritan work ethic and sense of social responsibility, respect for individual dignity, and voluntary individual submission to ever more complex social and political institutions. Parts of this combination may be found in non-Western cultures as well, for instance a puritan work ethic in Confucianism. Yet because of its primary loyalty to family ties, that creed was—and still is—deficient in social responsibility compared with the Judeo-Christian outreach to *all* neighbors. The comparative development of Western skills and goals should be a major theme of a world history course. Obviously, they are imperfectly practiced in Western culture (and, sadly, in decline as well). But how can we build a rational world order without them?

II. In pursuit of an answer to that question, responsible world history begins with the present; we should first take our students around the world with the help of current headlines. As the news shows, we live in a tightly packed interdependent world, unified by Western power and, with the help of many non-Westerners, functioning according to Western (or even American) patterns of conducting business and international relations. For better or worse, Western accomplishments have become the universal norm in weapons, science, technology, state organization, economic productivity, and popular culture. As any globetrotter can testify, Western life and cultural tastes—all too often in their most superficial forms—provide the irresistible model guiding the imagination and policies of all non-Western countries and people, even where officially repudiated, as among Islamic fundamentalists. In this Westernized world non-Western people are now testing what contribution their indigenous cultural resources can make for the common benefit. (Teachers and students may cite current examples in medicine, the arts, or religion.)

In this context one tragic fact stands out: under the Western impact all non-Western people, except for the Japanese (whose exceptionality deserves special treatment), have lost the sovereignty of cultural continuity. They are caught in profoundly divisive cultural disorientation. On the one hand, they desire to preserve their traditions (now generally interpreted in subtly idealized Westernized forms and communicated by means of Western media). On the other, they aspire to Western standards of living and global respectability with the help of all available Western instruments of power, eager to be counted in the world. By contrast, the countries of the West still enjoy the consensus-fostering benefits of cultural continuity reaffirmed by worldwide preeminence, even while increasingly infiltrated by non-Western ways.

Our world now is an interdependent economic and political system dominated by the major countries of North America, Western Europe, and a Westernized East Asia, which inevitably introduces a Western slant into world history. It is a framework filled with intense conflict between rich and poor, well-fed and starving, culturally secure and culturally splintered, powerful and helpless; neighborhoods and regions are bitterly divided over religion, race, ethnicity, and languages. Violence, often in the most inhumane forms, is widespread. In addition, the world's population is rapidly increasing, adding to the ecological strains imposed on nature's bounties. These facts can be easily related to current issues in world politics culled from the news.

The main point should be to stress our own involvement in the state of the world. Our country, with its complex problems, is set into tension-ridden global interdependence. That battered world is the framework for our students' lives. They must assess their personal prospects and define their identity as individuals and citizens within the constraints of that global interdependence. This framework also applies to a meaningful history course designed to help students—and ourselves too, as teachers—make sense of the problems that now and in the foreseeable future trouble our lives individually and collectively.

This expanded assessment of the present could well be the most effective starting point for the proper study of world history. How then to organize and interpret the mind-boggling vastness of the human past for a world history survey?

III. My suggestion would be to start with the Fertile Crescent, India, and ancient China, the early centers of cultural creativity, always stressing the influence of geography, the most important determinant of cultural development. An outline of the human accomplishments in these lands should include the emergence of religion (or religious philosophy) out of war-torn perilous times: Buddhism, Hinduism, Confucianism, and Jewish monotheism, together with their mutual contact through trade. Next come Greece, the Roman Empire, and the rise of Christianity, to be followed by a brief account of the rise and fall of the chief empires in the open Eurasian space: Persian, Arabian, Mongolian, and Turkish (to show, for example, that expansionism is not a peculiarity of Western culture but is a basic human trait, displayed in African or Amerindian history as well); the Arab story, of course, includes the emergence and spread of Islam. In each case attention should be called to the strengths and weaknesses of these empires, to their cultural resources, to their extensive trade networks, as well as to their contribution to Western culture. Columbus's stumbling upon the Western hemisphere offers a special opportunity for a comparative look at the accomplishments and traditions of the Amerindian people prior to their domination by European weapons and diseases.

Then follows the rise of Western Europe, with explanations why exceptionally favorable conditions beyond human control contributed to turn that part of the world into a cultural greenhouse in which keen competitive diversity was enhanced by a common cultural tradition. A brief survey of the evolution of Western power and culture would help to explain the success of European expansionism that, by the twentieth century, had created a Westernized world.

Next I would emphasize the fateful consequences of Western expansionism, pointing to its ecological, medical, economic, political, and cultural effects around the world. Students should discuss select case studies from East and South Asia, the Middle East, Africa, and the Western Hemisphere, showing the destruction of the original cultural integrity, the miseries that followed, and the beginning rebellion, under Western inspiration, against colonialism. Time permitting, this section might be enriched by a discussion of theories of imperialism and anti-imperialism. In any case, special attention should again be given to the exceptional case of Japan.

Having moved into the twentieth century, I would call attention to the fast technological advance, the new intensity of worldwide communications, the quadrupling of the world's population, and the resulting threats to the environment. I would especially stress the extreme violence and inhumanity caused by the extension of European power politics around the world in the wake of World War I. The Allied victory in 1918, popularizing the ideals of freedom, democracy, and equality, led to the mobilization of raw masses of people in the defeated countries, and subsequently throughout Asia and Africa, for participation in the competition for global power. In this deadly game the West, led by the United States, proudly set the universal model, thereby also becoming burdened—by the refined moral sensibility here advocated—with the responsibility for the consequences.

Our students certainly need an objective analysis of totalitarianism as an effort to organize utterly unprepared masses of people in Russian Eurasia, Italy, Germany, and eventually also in China, for catching up to the Western model. What in the leading Western countries has been achieved over centuries by largely voluntary cooperation had to be matched in the shortest time possible by all-inclusive political organization, by total reculturation, as in Stalin's Soviet Union. The human fury and technical perfection of weapons growing out of World War I soon led to the unprecedented destruction of human life in World War II, at the end of which the United States emerged as the foremost superpower matched superficially by the Soviet Union. Students should be made aware of that war's human cost.

I would then briefly describe the new world order of ever-intensifying global interdependence emerging after 1945, as the framework of the violence-prone political history of the world to the present. I would pay due attention to the nuclear arms race in the cold war and to the formation of non-Western states after the Western model, all drawn into the global competition with scant success. Totalitarian controls, like the more modest experiments of "modernization" and "development" have failed to overcome the tragic inequalities of cultural resources produced by unequal natural circumstances around the world. The rich have turned richer and the poor poorer both in political power and standards of living, as can easily be illustrated from current events. In this survey the role of the United Nations, the surge of post-1945 Japan, the rise of Israel, communism in China, and the collapse of the Soviet Union under Gorbachev deserve examination.

IV. Having come home to the present and trying, in conclusion, to draw the most fundamental forward-looking lessons from taking a long backward look, I would argue that humanity has now entered an utterly unprecedented new era. In this age of global confluence all people of the world, despite the immense differences in their cultural conditioning, languages, religions, and political organizations, have been tightly compacted into inescapable competitive interaction. They have become infinitely more visible to each other in instant communication and envious comparison than in any previous world system; yet they still do not understand how to overcome the cultural barriers that divide them. Now all past guidelines are in need of modification. What counts in this enlarged scale of human existence are more inclusive views within the global framework.

As a meaningful world history shows, past routines of life were shaped by small—and sometimes very small—communities. Now the people of the world have to learn how to adjust realistically to the burdens of global interdependence. That adjustment is difficult even for powerful Westerners used to the extensive (but largely unconscious) discipline of managing their complex societies; many of them already feel overloaded, unwilling and unable to change their ways. Global vision is even more difficult for the rapidly multiplying people barely surviving in the poor lands of the world.

Whatever the obstacles, the mastery of the human skills and attitudes needed for greater equality and peaceful cooperation in our worldwide interdependence take precedence over cultural diversity. What counts in this endeavor is not technological progress, nor consumerist self-indulgence, but concentration on the complex skills of human relations, an intensified moral and intellectual dedication to the subtle arts of peaceful cooperation. How can we prepare ourselves for the twenty-first century unless we help to build a common human ground for worldwide cooperation? The logic of world-shrinking interdependence leaves no other way.

These arguments—suitably geared to various levels of instruction—offer ample opportunity for discussion and clarification. May they help to devise world history courses capable of serving the needs of our unprecedented new era in human existence!

The World Outside the West Course Sequence at Stanford University

James Lance and Richard Roberts ◆ March 1991

For a more detailed discussion of The World Outside the West course sequence, please refer to Richard Roberts, "Teaching Non-Western History at Stanford," in Learning History in America: Schools, Cultures, and Politics, *edited by Lloyd Kramer, Donald Reid, and William Barney (Minneapolis: Univ. of Minnesota Press, 1994), pp. 53–70.*

◆ ◆ ◆ ◆

In an increasingly interdependent, multinational, and multicultural world, familiarity with the background, concerns, and problems of societies other than those spawned from the Western tradition has become a present and growing imperative of modern life. Stanford University undergraduates are required to take a year-long Western culture sequence and at least one course on a non-Western culture. This requirement, which was mandated by the Stanford Faculty Senate to take effect in 1980, reintroduced the required Western culture after a hiatus of ten years. (In 1986–87, the Faculty Senate revised its Western culture requirement to reflect demographic and intellectual changes by mandating the inclusion of at least one non-European culture and reducing the significance of the "core" reading list. The collective name of the various tracks was changed to CIV—cultures, ideas, and values. These new courses were introduced first in the fall quarter, 1989–90.)

The non-Western culture requirement—one course as opposed to three quarters for Western culture—reflected faculty concern that if nearly all United States students lack an acquaintance with the Western tradition, their knowledge of the world outside the West is even more limited. The rationale behind the non-Western requirement was clear: five-sixths of the world's population and four-fifths of the world's sovereign nations are located *outside* of Europe and those areas of European settlement considered extensions of the West (the United States, Canada, Australia, and New Zealand). For at least the past forty years, military conflict and economic development in the non-Western world have arguably had a greater impact upon American society than have events taking place in Europe.

Incorporating the non-Western requirement into the existing curriculum presented few difficulties. At Stanford, there are well over 100 humanities and social science faculty specializing in Africa, East Asia,

Latin America, and other parts of the non-Western world. Students may satisfy the non-Western requirement by taking any one of about fifty-five designated courses. Most of these courses are designed to introduce students to a particular world area, culture, or society through the perspective of a particular discipline, for example: contemporary African politics, traditional Chinese literature, or the history of colonial Mexico.

In the early 1980s, a group of non-Western area studies faculty proposed a new course sequence, The World Outside the West. Where this sequence differed from other non-Western courses was in its interdisciplinary and cross-cultural emphasis. The course was to be taught by a team of area specialists—for example, anthropologists, historians, and political scientists—and would be aimed primarily at sophomores and juniors desirous of fulfilling the non-Western culture requirements.

Those of us proposing this new course were concerned that an unspecified one-quarter, non-Western culture course would not adequately portray the tremendous cultural and social diversity in the non-Western world, and we were dissatisfied with the "high" cultural emphasis implicit in the teaching of the "Western" culture requirement. We proposed, instead, a comparative study of three non-Western cultures over a two-quarter sequence, focusing on a broader definition of "culture." In this course, "culture" was conceived as lived experience, thus emphasizing social history. Since there were no ready-made models for such a course, we spent considerable time exploring alternative ways of conceptualizing and organizing the material we hoped to include in the course and in developing a model of culture that could be used as part of a debate with the proponents of Western "culture" as commonly conceived. We found Fernand Braudel's division of time into natural, social, and eventful time, as developed in his *The Mediterranean and the Mediterranean World of Philip II,* provocative and helpful in shaping the agenda for organizing course materials.

As our thinking evolved, the course came to concentrate on aspects of selected cultures in Asia (China), Africa (Nigeria), and the Americas (Mexico), and was to have a threefold objective: introduce students to a select number of non-Western cultures before and after extensive contact with the West; help students better understand the values, attitudes, and institutions of non-Western peoples in the modern world; and, furnish students with a framework for comparing and contrasting all cultures, including that of the West, thereby heightening students' sensitivity and appreciation of the varieties of human experience.

Students would not be the only beneficiaries of the course. The process of course development would present opportunities for enhanced dialogue among faculty who specialize in the study of non-Western societies. We expected this dialogue to encourage greater sensitivity to the comparative dimension in courses taught in our own fields of specialization and to generate insights into further innovation in the curriculum in regard to introductory courses in specific non-Western areas.

Teaching The World Outside the West began in the autumn of 1984–85 with funding from the Mellon Foundation and the National Endowment for the Humanities. From the outset, the faculty team, composed of two anthropologists, three historians, and a political scientist, had to confront and resolve two critical intellectual problems. One was to see how the various parts of each of the cultures with which they dealt could be presented in such a fashion as to render these parts into an interrelated, coherent, and apprehensible whole. The second problem was to shape the issues of the course—for the peoples of China, Nigeria, and Mexico—into a common and shared discourse. Tackling the first problem required development of intra-cultural understanding; handling the second necessitated trans-cultural comparison.

The faculty involved were convinced that the best way to confront the basic epistemological difficulties of the course was to present an overall and unifying analytic framework that stressed how men and women in different cultural areas responded to common problems relating to human efforts to control both nature and cosmic forces, and how these efforts shaped the society, economy, and polity. Particularly in the first quarter, where these three cultures are studied prior to sustained contact with the "West," we wanted to portray these cultures as dynamic and changing, in order to avoid the stereotype of the "changeless" non-Western world. We paid special attention to the social, economic, political, and intellectual feedback between natural time and social time. Although we began with detailed discussions of physical and human geography, we spent considerable time examining the indigenous world view—the bodies of philosophical, social, and religious thought—in each of the three cultures. The course came to be structured around an examination of what, explicitly, these indigenous bodies of thought express and how they are linked to social, economic, and political organization and change.

The professors' pedagogic goals were to analyze, mediate, and compare these bodies of thought, and to specify how peoples use these bodies of thought to inform, shape, and construct their various cultures. Central to our comparative approach was that these very different cultures were alternative responses to problems all human societies seek to resolve.

This comparative concept—different responses to common problems—helped organize the syllabus, lectures, and reading assignments. The goal here was to get students to appreciate that the great diversity of human cultures reflects the enormous creativity of human beings in their responses to problems and opportunities. We expected that students would come to see that the Western tradition is just one possibility among many. As a result, students would come to adopt a more detached perspective on their own culture.

While none of the faculty agreed on a common definition of culture, there was general concurrence that culture should include the schemes of perception, conception, and social action shared by members of a society in their quest to relate to each other and to make sense out of the universe in which they live. The concept of culture emphasized in the course would include the "Great Traditions" of art, literature, religion, and philosophy, dealing with these not as eternal and immutable verities, but as part of the everyday structures of life—including birth, rites of passage, marriage, and death. The course depicted culture as a fluid phenomenon, and solidly rejected the assumption usually made in connection with non-Western societies, that their cultures, once established, remain essentially unchanged thereafter.

Teachers presented both exogenous and endogenous views of the societies being studied in the course. Ethnographies, travelers' accounts, and similar documents imparted a sense of how these societies were viewed by outsiders, while views produced within the cultures themselves, entrenched, for example, in written or oral traditions, imparted a sense of how members of the societies perceived themselves. Faculty considered this emphasis on a dual perspective one of the main tasks of the course, for it would encourage students in the idea that any society can be regarded from a number of viewpoints and that social truth is relative. Regarding non-Western societies only in terms of Western concepts discourages appreciation of many of the cultural nuances essential to those societies and blinds one to their dynamism and creativity.

The faculty believed it imperative to stress in their teaching the immense variety of non-Western societies and cultural traditions. They wanted to sensitize students to the distortions of complex social realities that arise with the use of terms like "non-Western world" or "Third World," which are residual categories indicating not what various cultures are, but what they are not. Such terms not only suggest an unfounded degree of homogeneity in the world outside the West, they have also come to imply backwardness, poverty, and inscrutability. Placing emphasis on the heterogeneity of the non-Western world would indicate the falsification involved in indiscriminate use of such all-encompassing terms like "Third World" and would suggest further why the responses of non-Western peoples to Western intrusion have varied enormously from place to place.

The World Outside the West is a two-quarter sequence. The initial segment of the course deals with the societies of China, Mexico, and Nigeria before their enduring contact with an aggressive and interventionist West. The instructors' main objective during the opening quarter is to challenge stereotypical notions of presumably dormant and stagnant non-Western societies that became dynamic only after being energized through contact with the West. The lessons of this part of the course sequence are that many non-Western societies have traditions as complex, and in some cases lengthier, than those of the West and that there are no societies without their own sense of time.

For the instructors involved in the presentation of Chinese society and culture before extensive contact with the West, teaching focuses on some of the major elements that characterized the Chinese outlook, illustrating the ways in which a widely-shared, specifically Chinese world view was manifested in social, economic, and political arenas. Elements stressed include: the absence of a creation myth—that while the emergence of civilized, humane society may need explaining, the world itself simply is and cosmogony is not a serious issue; the view that the cosmos, the human/social realm, and the ordinary world around the Chinese are part of one holistic entity; the closely-related idea that this differentiated and hierarchical whole functions organically, so that conditions in one realm affect what happens in that of another; the emphasis in Chinese thought upon eclecticism, complementarity, and harmony rather than upon exclusivity, contradiction, and struggle; the predilection among Chinese not to divide what one thinks or knows from what one does—knowledge and action are but two sides of the same coin; and, the absence of a self-conscious science, which did not prevent the Chinese from developing a rich tradition of scientific and technological discovery.

Religion receives great emphasis in the examination of the central Mexican Aztec civilization. Teaching centers on the ways in which all aspects of what have been traditionally considered the religious aspects of culture—cosmology, pantheon, priesthood, ritualism, sacrifice, symbolism, sacred sites, architecture, pilgrimages, mythology, divination, magic, and theological and philosophical speculation—were elaborately developed and closely integrated with social and political organization, ethics, art aesthetics, literacy, and daily life. Partly through original documents, students are introduced to the central Mexican world view: they read Aztec philosophical poetry and confront the rudiments of the complicated and sophisticated Aztec calendar. The intimate interweaving of religion with daily life is important for understanding the Spanish conquest of Mexico, for the Aztecs regarded Cortés as a fulfillment of a prophecy that foretold the end of a political-cosmological cycle. Thus, the Aztec defeat cannot be comprehended without reference to Aztec religion and the interaction between Aztec and Spanish world views.

In regard to Nigeria, with the exception of the Islamic tradition to the north, the relatively small scale of most Nigerian societies hindered the development of a professional "intellectual" class. Lacking literacy, precolonial Nigerians did not bequeath to posterity a written corpus of philosophical traditions. The smallness of scale of many of the societies of Nigeria contributed to an intimacy of belief, analysis, and practice. Thus, it becomes extremely difficult, if not impossible, to separate religious thought from ethical behavior, philosophical traditions from political ideas. The Nigerians' complex cosmology, for example, demonstrates their understanding of causality and consequence. Problems of human survival demand a careful and continuous accounting to the spiritual world and the maintenance of balance within it. Examination of the Nigerian life cycle explores the closeness of the past, present, and future in the consciousness of Nigerians and in their religious thought. Throughout the Nigerian segment of the opening quarter, instruction hinges upon this critical sense of intimacy between thought and lived experience.

The second quarter of the course concentrates on the interaction of the three non-Western cultures/societies with the aggressive, curious, expansionist, and interventionist West. In keeping with the religious, philosophical, and cosmological themes of the opening quarter of the sequence, attention is directed toward the response of Christian Europeans (especially missionaries) to the religious ideas and values of the three societies and the responses of the peoples in these societies to the cosmology and ethical norms of the Christians in their midst. The course also addresses questions of how a society like China, with varying degrees of success, maintained its political independence in the face of Western pressure while at the same time it attempted to create new cultural syntheses between Western civilization and its own heritage. In its examination of the range of non-Western reactions to the West, the course reiterates its emphasis on the vast heterogeneity of the world outside the West. Discussion of the reactions of non-Western peoples to the West also reveals their deep ambivalence toward the West, an ambivalence that is one of the inescapable yet most important facts about the contemporary world.

The China portion of the second quarter addresses the issue of how Chinese social and religious thinking did or did not change in response to the intrusion of new modes and models of thought from the West. Lectures and readings cover the missionary movement in China and Chinese reaction to it, the confrontation of traditional ethical systems with rationalistic Western social theories, and the transformation of Marxism into a Maoist synthesis. In general, although the Chinese intelligentsia were exposed to Christianity, they found its message inadequate. They were more accepting of a wide variety of Western secular philosophies, materialist or positivist in character, ranging from Social Darwinism to Marxism-Leninism. Why there was a general embracing of Western secular thought forms one of the principal questions of the second quarter Chinese section. In seeking to find answers to this question, efforts are made to sensitize students to what is universal and what is parochial in Western thought.

The beginning of the second quarter Mexico segment discusses the conquest and colonization of Mexico in terms of the philosophical debates about human nature that the New World inspired in Spanish conquistadores and missionaries. The main subject of debate was whether, and if so to what degree, the indigenous peoples of the New World were fully human, having intellectual capabilities of a level sufficient enough for them to become completely Christian. The enslavers and exploiters argued that Indians, although descendants of Adam and Eve, had devolved to such an extent that they were in essence beasts. Protectors of the Indians argued that they were just like Adam and Eve immediately after expulsion from Paradise and that therefore Indians were ready for full-scale evangelization. From discussions of debates and policies in regard to the Indians, the segment concludes with an examination of the politics, policies, and challenges facing the various Mexican governments during the nineteenth and twentieth centuries.

Second quarter lectures and readings on the peoples of Nigeria concentrate on the quite different responses to Christianity among the followers of Islam and those adhering to "animist" beliefs. The argument presented in the segment is that the many similarities between Islam and Christianity, coupled with the long history of conflict between the two world religions, enabled Muslims to successfully resist the proselytizing efforts of Christian missionaries. The intense linkage of localized animist beliefs with the maintenance of a local small-scale political order, however, created special opportunities for Christian missionary efforts, particularly on the heels of European military conquest. The effects on small-scale Nigerian societies of the confrontation between Christianity and animism are graphically portrayed in Achebe's *Things Fall Apart*. Although rejection or acceptance of Christianity were the most potent alternatives available to Nigerians in their encounter with this aspect of Western intrusion, they were not the only ones. The segment examines instances of syncretic responses to Christianity, such as the Cherubim and Seraphim movement and the efforts of Nigerians to establish an independent Nigerian Christian Church. Studying these syncretic movements accentuates the creativity and dynamism of Nigerian societies in their reactions to the West.

The World Outside the West sequence was much neater and tidier on paper than it actually was in the classroom. China, Mexico, and Nigeria were very different cultures, with considerably different historiographical traditions. Moreover, neither Mexico nor Nigeria were recognized precolonial entities. This required that we redefine the units of study: for the first quarter, Mexico was essentially the valley of Mexico; for Nigeria, we had to balance two quite different narratives, one for the northern Muslim Hausa and the other for the acephalous Igbo of the southeast. While the teachers of China and Mexico presented more unitary views of their respective cultures and societies, teachers of Nigeria tried to present the range of diversity in what was to become Nigeria. The Hausa and the Igbo were chosen because they were the principal players in the Nigerian civil war of the late 1960s.

Part of the problem for both teachers and students was the unevenness in the presentations of these regions and in the quality of the literature available. Much more and much better introductory material was available for China and Mexico than for Nigeria. However, the novels and other readings (including Achebe's *Things Fall Apart* and the wonderful autobiography of a Hausa woman, *Baba of Karo*) more than favored the Nigerian side. The course therefore avoided the problems of "equivalences" by acknowledging to students the very different historiographical traditions in the three regions. But other forms of "equivalences" continued to plague the course.

Chronology was one such problem. Events occurred at very different times in each of these areas, as did the point of sustained contact with the West, which was to serve as the transition from the first to the second quarter. Although somewhat awkward for students, we agreed on what we call "conceptual" time, in which comparable events occurred. Thus, the establishment of the Aztec state could be compared to the Ming/Ch'ing transition in China, which was parallel to the consolidation of power by Muslim rulers in Hausaland. Similarly, the transition from the first to the second quarter also followed "conceptual" time, wherein the Spanish conquest of Mexico could be compared to the treaty port system in China and to the British abolition of the slave trade and the beginning of colonial conquest in Nigeria.

The most intractable problem we have faced in five years of teaching The World Outside the West has been that of recruiting faculty. This course is extremely labor intensive, involving three faculty for each of two quarters. Thus, finding two faculty for each of the three areas covered—or finding one prepared to teach both quarters—has been a daunting task. Central to the conceptualization of the course, however, was our expectation that the areas included would change over time, but that we would always try to have three different cultures. For the first two years, we included China, Mexico, and Nigeria. The next year, we switched from Mexico to Peru, but retained China and Nigeria. Given faculty leave patterns, we then returned to the original grouping, only to plan for another change for 1989–90 (Egypt, Japan, and Nigeria as the three cultures "outside the West").

Despite the administrative burdens of long-range planning and the substitution of new areas, these changes have kept the course material fresh. We have to rethink the issues each time we teach, and in the process, we also come a little closer to understanding better the diversity of cultures throughout the world and how to teach about them.

The World Outside the West is not designed to be a "world history" course. It is designed to expose students to ranges of diversity in three deeply studied parts of the world and to challenge them to think critically about these areas in relationship to one another and in relationship to the West. The course has a reputation among students as being extremely demanding, but also quite rewarding.

Some Thoughts About the Stanford Course The World Outside the West

Lanny Fields ◆ March 1991

In the past few decades, there has been a concerted effort by American universities to offer courses in non-Western history. This effort is part of a larger perspective made more pressing as a result of United States dominance in the world after 1945. The expansion of communism in Eurasia as well as the appearance of trouble spots in Africa, the Americas, and Asia infused this view with urgency. As more experts on non-Western societies appeared, the tendencies to see these areas as mere extensions of the West or as passive receptacles for Western actions or dominations began to be challenged. Yet many Western civilization texts overemphasized Western societies and experiences and then merely offered a chapter or two on non-Western cultures. In recent years, however, new efforts to correct Eurocentric imbalances in university courses have surfaced.

At Stanford University in the 1980s, the faculty mandated that a variety of non-Western courses be taught. The World Outside the West is one of these courses and deserves serious consideration as a model for others.

The World Outside the West combines crucial elements and techniques needed to teach general education courses effectively:

1) It is cross-culturally centered—Cross-cultural courses have the potential to excite students because they examine different cultures and thus expose similarities in the ways problems are approached. Such revelations can affect students in a way comparable to the impact alien cultures had on early explorers. For example, I have noticed how intrigued students can become upon seeing how the Han Chinese and the Romans treated the "barbarians" who threatened their frontiers. Stimulating discussions have been sparked by this and other comparisons.

2) Interdisciplinary—Interdisciplinary approaches are valuable because they enable students to witness how different academic disciplines regard topics.

3) Team taught—Team teaching is especially rewarding. Faculty members must discuss (as the Stanford people did at length) a course's educational objectives, conceptual schemes, and analytic modes. Team teaching, of course, often exposes students to varied teaching styles: lecturing, Socratic discussion and discovery, the use of slides, films, or representative artifacts. It has been my experience that interactive teaching is especially rewarding in a team-teaching format. In this approach, all faculty members are present at each session and may be expected to interject their perspectives about a given topic. In addition, some classes lend themselves to role-playing by the instructors.

Used selectively and with careful preparation, such techniques can bring history to life.

The teachers of The World Outside the West also should be commended for interchanging different cultural groups beyond Aztec Mexico, Nigeria, and China. This result enabled them to examine new approaches and themes. Replacing China with Japan, for example, might cause them to address the consequences of long-term military rule or the significance of foreign influence. This keeps the course fresh for the instructors, and more important, it offers them added and varied insights that inevitably broaden their horizons and improve their ability to teach the course ever more effectively.

The Stanford team also addressed such problems as faculty staffing difficulties, which is helpful to their peers at other institutions who who need to learn the positive and negative aspects of these non-Western courses.

Evaluation of students, a vital but thorny topic, should also have been considered. Questions remain as to whether they did employ essay examinations or multiple-choice tests? Whether papers were assigned? Did they have book quizzes or discussions? How large were the classes? Class size may be a significant determinant of the evaluation measure.

My major reservation about The World Outside the West course is its Eurocentric bias. This is not to say that the Stanford group failed to grapple with the problem. They correctly note that "regarding non-Western societies only in terms of Western concepts discourages appreciation of many of the cultural nuances essential to those societies." I could not agree more, yet the structure of the course sequences themselves reveals Western-derived or baseline expectations.

The structural orientation of the two-course sequence is Western. Certainly the Stanford team wants to reject stereotypical Western perspectives about these cultures; nevertheless the attempt to show change-driven people is clearly Western. Change, dynamic institutions, not to say notions of progress, imply Western orientations. What if a society does not change appreciably over time? What if it views itself as unchanging or stable? If these perspectives shape a culture's self-image, our duty as teachers is to understand them on their own terms, not as we would like them to be. The dynamic, transforming, progressive West seems to be looming in the intellectual background of such courses. Phrases like "absence of a creation myth" or "absence of a self-conscious science" appear in the explication of The World Outside the West course. "Absence" implies that the ideal culture must possess a creation myth or a self-conscious science. I begin my world civilizations courses with a discussion of the biases that inform the study and teaching of such courses. One topic is the Eurocentric world view. We explore terminology (Far East, Middle East), for example, to learn how we in the West look at the world through cultural lenses. One needs to undergo a continual self analysis and a process of introspection along with one's students to rid the curriculum (as far as it is possible) of ideas and terminology that are European-derived. Such an effort, though imperfect, can help us understand the Jains or the Han Chinese on their own terms rather than through a biased viewpoint. Without this awareness and criticism, we are doomed to misunderstanding non-Western people.

The second World Outside the West sequence necessarily regards each society in the context of its interactive experiences with Western countries. While there is an attempt to examine internal cultural elements and their independent developments (especially with regard to China), the overwhelming thrust of the presentation is to see these cultures through Western prisms. A related and serious problem of this approach is the degree of Western uniformity. How similar or different are Portuguese merchants and British missionaries? Would it not be beneficial for students to examine what the West is? Are there many Wests? Such a discussion about what the "West" means would highlight some problems in teaching and learning when one operates at a dangerous level of generalization.

One interesting practice of the Stanford team is its use of missionary records. This might offer frameworks for comparisons and contrasts with reference to the Westerners and the Aztecs or the Chinese. One might examine the relationship between the political might and ideological mission work. The Chinese often tried to persuade their Muslim subjects about the benefits of Confucianism in a manner not unlike the French Catholics in southern China. Still, the missionaries' records offer yet another Western framework for misunderstanding non-Western cultures. In this regard, perhaps an examination of the Mayans rather than the Aztecs might offer a less biased view of Meso-American society. Perspectives about the Aztecs have often been influenced by sources from Westerners who arrived in the New World after Columbus. Views of the Mayans, on the other hand, have been derived from archaeologists, anthropologists, and linguists who, we might safely presume, are less apt to be prejudiced about their subjects.

The teachers of The World Outside the West are sensitive to the problems inherent in offering a non-Western course. Some of these issues are perhaps unresolvable as Westerners learn about non-Westerners; yet it is essential to the learning process that we, students and teachers, seek to know people on their own terms rather than as Westerners or as non-Westerners. At least by discussing these concerns with our students we help sensitize them to the severe obstacles as well as to the sublime joys of learning about people other than themselves. And the pleasures of learning as seen on students' faces or heard in their voices when they ask questions can offer the teacher a lovely reward that may endure for a day, or perhaps a lifetime.

Teaching World History

William H. McNeill ◆ March 1991

What can a teacher do with the buzzing, blooming confusion that is world history? The problem is twofold. On the one hand, the subject is infinite. On the other hand, considerable attention must be paid to the heritage of Western civilization that shaped American institutions and made the country what it is. Mere confusion will inevitably result from an indiscriminate effort to deal with everything we know about the past; and if too little emphasis is placed on the world-transforming character of Western civilization throughout the past 500 years, then our heritage from that truly remarkable epoch of world history will be inexcusably undervalued. As yet, there are no generally agreed-upon models; historians have only recently begun to try to frame a coherent vision of the history of the world.

Yet the imperatives pointing toward a world history are obvious. In the first place, our country has become part of an intensely interactive world system that no longer revolves solely upon events in Europe, as was (or at least seemed to be) the case as recently as the 1930s. To deal effectively with Asians, Africans, Latin Americans, and Europeans we need to know how the historical past has shaped their diverse outlooks upon the world. In the second place, migrants from Asia, Africa, and Latin America have filled our classrooms with students whose ethnic and cultural background is not "Western." They need a past they can share with Americans of European descent; and equally, Americans of European descent need a past they can share with all their fellow citizens, including the indigenous Indian population that got here before anyone else. World history fits these needs, and only world history can hope to do so.

How then should the history of the human adventure on earth be presented in our classrooms? We need a clear and distinct idea about what matters most. Teachers might rely on a few simple rules of thumb:

1) Human power and wealth have increased through time because people strive for them. People are perpetually on the lookout for new skills or ideas that will increase their wealth or power. Borrowing interesting new capabilities from strangers may upset existing relationships, it may arouse in some the desire to maintain local practices undefiled, and it may hurt some people while it benefits others. Still, the changeability of human history results from the modification of established ways of thinking and acting provoked most often by contacts with strangers.

2) People are often unaware of the consequences and implications of particular actions or choices, so that human purposes are a very imperfect guide to what actually occurs. Side effects regularly distort purposes. Multiple causes are everywhere, and so are cross purposes. The open-endedness of human experience needs continual emphasis to counteract the tendency to treat whatever did happen as somehow foreordained.

3) Students should try to make moral judgments about the past, but only after they have thought about the norms and expectations that prevailed among those being judged. Students need to know that human beings make sense of their lives by striving to conform to the norms of behavior that group membership imposes on them.

These rules of thumb about how to approach human history still do not answer the practical question of how to distribute classroom time among the infinite possibilities that world history offers. Two overarching goals should guide decision making.

First, students need to realize that they share the earth with people whose beliefs and actions are different from their own and arise from divergent cultural heritages. The way to make this clear is to define as fully and richly as possible the distinctive national traditions of the United States, and then to sample other cultural traditions, choosing for closer study those cultures of importance for global affairs in our time. Schools must therefore teach both the national history of the United States and the history of the rest of the world, paying special attention to the principal civilizations of Eurasia (including that of Western Europe) because they shaped the world views of the majority of human beings today. Africa, Latin America, and North America, as well as Eurasia came to share in the European heritage owing to the same processes of expansion that operated within Eurasia itself.

Second, students need to know that the various cultures and different civilizations that divide humanity are all part of a larger process of historical development whereby successful ideas and skills, wherever initiated, spread from people to people and culture to culture. Elaboration and diffusion of skills are as old as the emergence of humanity, whose distinctive trait is learning how to do things from others. Finds of obsidian and other scarce minerals in places remote from their origin show that Paleolithic hunters communicated across long distances. In subsequent ages, trading and raiding, missionary enterprise and mere wandering linked communities. This means that the One World of our time is not new. The speed of communication and rapidity of reaction have increased enormously, but the process of innovation and diffusion of skills is age old.

Indeed that is what defines the pattern of world history as distinct from the pattern of more local histories, including the history of separate civilizations. Accordingly, world history ought to be more organized around major breakthroughs in communication that, step-by-step, intensified interactions within ever larger regions of the earth until instant global communications became the pervasive reality of our own time. By focusing on the pattern of interaction, and showing how borrowed skills and ideas always had to be adapted to fit local geographical and cultural environments, a simple and commonsensical pattern for world history emerges within which detailed study of any chosen time and place will fit smoothly.

The course of study should begin with a sampling of the culture of preliterate societies. Hunters and gatherers and autonomous villages of food producers prevailed in the distant past. A few such societies survived into modern times, allowing anthropologists to study them with insight and sympathy. That insight can and should be communicated to students just because their lives are set in an utterly different sort of social environment. But this can only be preliminary. The major focus of attention must be upon the major civilization of Eurasia.

Studying European, Chinese, Indian, and Middle Eastern civilizations with sufficient sympathy to be able to present their ideas and institutions, so to speak, "from the inside" is a formidable task. But art and literature—the "classics" of each civilization—are available, and even small excerpts from such classics can convey something of the spirit and distinctive flavor of the civilization in question. Looking at the reproductions of great works of art and reading translations from the world's great literature invites students to react as individuals to the treasures of the human past. That experience ought to be part of every course in world history.

But random sampling of the world classics will only create confusion. Teachers can simplify without unduly distorting the reality of the four principal Eurasian cultural traditions by showing how each was built around a master institution, with a ruling idea to match. For ancient Greece, the territorial state was the ruling institution and the matching idea was natural law, applicable both to humans within the polls and to inanimate nature. For China, the extended family and the notion of decorum played a similar organizing role for the behavior of human beings and of the cosmos. For India, the ruling institution was caste and the organizing idea was transcendentalism, that is, the reality of the spiritual realm above and beyond the illusory world of sense. And for the Middle East, bureaucratic monarchy and monotheism played the same organizing roles.

Obviously, these four separate institutional-and-idea systems mingled through subsequent time. Thus, with the rise of the Roman empire and spread of Christianity, European civilization blended the Middle Eastern and part of the Indian with its Greek heritage. Similarly, China, Japan, and the adjacent East Asian people borrowed a great deal of the Indian heritage when Buddhism spread to that part of the world. Middle Easterners combined the Greek heritage with their own after Alexander's conquests and borrowed Indian transcendentalism a few centuries later. India, likewise, toyed with Middle Eastern ideas of bureaucratic monarchy as early as the third century B.C., and explored the full complexity of both Middle Eastern and European civilizations after 1000, when first Moslem and then European conquerors intruded upon Hindu society as a new ruling caste.

Because each of the major Eurasian civilizations took form long ago—before 400 B.C. in Western Eurasia and before 100 B.C. in East Asia—a course in world history must devote considerable emphasis to this classical, formative stage. But once a grasp of the enduring character of each civilization has been achieved, emphasis ought to shift to the processes of interaction across civilizational boundaries and the subsequent blending of what had begun as separate traditions.

Main landmarks of that process my be listed as follows:

1) The rise of cities, writing, and occupational specialization, centered initially in the Middle East. The impact of Middle Eastern skills and ideas extended all the way across Eurasia by 1500 B.C., when the Shang dynasty brought chariots and such characteristic ideas as the seven-day week to the valley of the Yellow River.

2) The opening of regular caravan connections between China and Rome, and between the Middle East and India, about 100 B.C. At about the same time, Mediterranean sailors discovered the monsoons of the Indian Ocean and began to participate in a much older sea-borne commercial network uniting the Indian Ocean with the South China Sea The so-called Silk Road was the most famous overland route, but the caravan world extended north and south of the Silk Road proper, and in common with the navigation of the southern seas, created a slender

Eurasian world market for luxury goods that could bear the cost of long-distance transport.

3) The development and spread of the so-called higher religions of Judaism, Buddhism, Christianity, and Islam between about 500 B.C. and A.D. 630. These faiths provided a moral universe that countered the injustices and impersonality of urban bureaucratic and hierarchical society by inviting their followers to create communities of believers wherever they found themselves. This stabilized human relations within the expanding Eurasian civilizations, and, through conscious and deliberate missionary activity, attracted neighboring peoples into the widening and ever-intensifying circles of interacting civilizations.

4) The large-scale domestication of camels after about A.D. 300. Caravans could now cross hot deserts, with the effect of bringing Arabia and West Africa into the interacting circles of civilizations. The Moslem Middle East became the principal center of the resulting system of trade and transport, and Moslem skills spread in every direction. In particular, Moslem merchants taught the rules of bazaar trading to the nomad world of the Eurasian steppe and also to the Chinese.

5) Cheap and dependable water transport resulted from technical advances in shipbuilding and, equally important, from the extensive canalization of rivers, especially in China. The horizon point of this development came about A.D. 1000 when long-distance trade ceased to be confined to luxuries, and began to alter everyday life for ordinary people because goods of common consumption could now bear the cost of transport across hundreds and even thousands of miles. In many ways, this represents the dawn of the modern age, as much or more than the familiar date of 1500. China was the principal center of the resulting intensification of exchanges and, like the Moslems before them, the Chinese swiftly developed skills superior to the rest of the world.

6) The establishment of the political unity throughout much of Eurasia by the Mongols in the thirteenth century. This was the principal medium for the diffusion of Chinese skills westward, for as the career of Marco Polo illustrates, the Mongol peace allowed literally thousands of people to move back and forth between China and the rest of the Eurasian world. Chinese skills therefore spread westward—notably gunpowder, printing, and the compass, three key technological elements in Europe's subsequent assumption of world leadership.

7) The familiar opening of the oceans by the Europeans just before and after 1500. European merchants established trading posts on the coasts and islands of the Indian Ocean and played an increasingly active part in the trade and politics of the southern seas and East and West Africa thereafter. In addition, the Americas entered abruptly into the circle of Eurasian interactions, exposing the Amerindians to

repeated disease disasters and allowing Europeans to establish thriving colonies in the New World. (From this point onward, the history of the United States becomes part of world history and ought to be treated as such. Some separate treatment of United States history is needed; but world history ought not to omit our national past. Instead, world history courses should put the national past in perspective.)

8) The tapping of mechanical power for industrial production and then for transport and communication, beginning in a dramatic way about 1750. From this time onward, the three-fold structure suggested in our ideal curriculum becomes a practicable guide for directing attention toward the most important traits of the modern age: (a) the democratic revolution in government; (b) the industrial revolution in economics; and (c) the demographic upsurge.

In studying this increasingly far-ranging and intensive interaction, the way each step prepared the way for the next is worth emphasizing. But as always, history is not a simple success story. Costs must be counted as well as gains. The loss of autonomy for local peoples and cultures that resulted from the arrival of powerful strangers in their midst was always the price of admission to the interacting circle of sophisticated skills and exchanges. Exposure to new and lethal infectious diseases was another cost of the civilizing process. Each expansion of the range of communications put new populations at risk, and the resulting die-off from the sudden onset of smallpox and other diseases regularly weakened local peoples and sometimes crippled or even destroyed them. The case of the American Indians is the most dramatic example, but Australians, Polynesians, and people of the Siberian forests suffered parallel disease disasters in modern times; and catastrophic disease encounters in earlier ages—the Black Death and the Antonine plagues—are also worth attention.

World history built along these lines can prepare students to live in the interactive world of the twenty-first century more serenely and wisely than would otherwise be possible for them. It would also give appropriate weight and attention to the primacy of Western civilization in the last 500 years.

Study of world history with the help of simple ideas like these can be an intellectually uplifting experience; it is also an essential preparation for citizenship. World history is therefore very much worth doing, and worth doing well. It belongs with the national history of our country at the core of K–12 social studies.

Regions and Civilizations

Remapping the West:
Teaching the Middle East in World
and Western Civilization Courses

Joel Beinin ◆ December 1992

Teaching Middle Eastern topics is often considered a uniquely problematic enterprise, hence the region is frequently avoided or minimized in Western civilization or world history courses in spite of the many links between Middle Eastern and European societies and the centrality of Islamic societies in the complex of Afro-Eurasian agrarian-based citied civilization. This essay considers themes from Middle Eastern history and Arabo-Islamic texts that might be incorporated into such survey courses. The 1979 Iranian Revolution, the 1991 Gulf War, and United States involvement in the Arab-Israeli conflict underscore the importance of knowing something about the historical and cultural traditions of a part of the world in which Americans have been and are likely to remain engaged for some time. But teachers will want to assure themselves that the incorporation of Middle Eastern themes can be undertaken and justified intellectually and pedagogically on other than purely pragmatic or presentist grounds.

The traditional genealogy of Western civilization locates its origins in the Hebrew Bible, ancient Greece and Rome, and the New Testament. Its developmental trajectory was interrupted during the medieval period, which Henri Pirenne argued was brought on by the rise of Islam. But it resumed with the scholastic philosophers, the Age of Exploration, the

Renaissance, the Reformation, the Enlightenment, the French and American revolutions, and the passing of the torch of progress across the Atlantic to the United States. (For a slightly different genealogy and critique see Eric Wolf, *Europe and the People Without History*. This narrative, especially in such a crude form, is problematic for several reasons. Annexing Greek civilization to Europe ignores its actual geographic location, which was as much Middle Eastern as European. The prominence of Spain in the rise of western Europe is displaced. Insofar as the entity being described is conceived as a Judeo-Christian civilization, it incorrectly regards Jewish culture as European, whereas from the rise of Islam to the fifteenth century, most of the important centers of Jewish culture, and indeed most Jews, were in the Muslim world. Arabic-speaking Jews from Mesopotamia, Spain, and Sicily often served as cultural mediators and translators from Greek to Arabic and from Arabic to Latin.

A more comprehensive conception that justifies including the Middle East in a course on Western civilization and provides a framework for locating Islamic societies in a world civilization course would be to consider the Mediterranean basin with an extension into the Iranian plateau as a zone of dynamic interaction among ancient Egyptian, Greek, Persian, Islamic, Jewish, and Christian cultural traditions supported by a commercial network in which the Middle East functioned as the chief entrepôt for long distance trade between South and East Asia and the Mediterranean region. This notion draws on the work of Fernand Braudel (especially *The Mediterranean and the Mediterranean World in the Age of Philip II*; S. D. Goiten's *A Mediterranean Society*, a multivolume history of the Jewish communities of the medieval Arab world based on the documents of the Cairo geniza; Marshall Hodgson's magisterial three-volume study, *The Venture of Islam*, and Janet L. Abu-Lughod's *Before European Hegemony: The World System*, A.D. *1250–1350*; and Amitav Ghosh's *In an Antique Land*, which is beautifully written and suitable for assignment to students. It helps us to understand that in the formation of what has come to be defined as Western culture Islamic societies functioned as mediators between the Hellenic tradition and western Europe during a period when Islam formed the cultural framework for long-distance trade around and beyond the Mediterranean basin. Thus, Mediterranean trade and the dialogue between the Socratic (Greek philosophical) and the Abrahamic (monotheistic) cultural traditions (the terms are Hodgson's) can be used to organize a discussion of the interaction between Islam and Christian Europe in the realm of economic and social history and literate high culture. Even in the realm of popular culture it is possible to find common themes and traditions traversing the Mediterranean, though local knowledge is generally more powerful in shaping popular culture than are broad regional influences.

When adding Middle Eastern themes and texts to existing courses, an obvious starting point is the rise of Islam and the Qur'an (Koran), the Muslim sacred book. According to the Qur'an, the God (Allah) who spoke to Muhammad (570–632) is the same God who spoke previously to Adam, Abraham, Moses, and Jesus. Altogether, some two dozen figures who appear in the Jewish and Christian scriptures are regarded as prophets in the Qur'an, which presents itself as the final revelation of God to humanity through his emissary Muhammad, the seal of the prophets. The *surahs* (chapters) of Joseph, Mary, and parts of The Cow exemplify the common narrative elements of the Hebrew Bible, the New Testament, and the Qur'an. They also highlight some important differences, for example the Muslim view that regarding Jesus as the son of God contradicts the unity of God, the fundamental theological doctrine of Islam. The *surahs* of The Cow and The Women reveal something of the flavor of the *shari`ah* (Islamic law), the defining framework for classical Islamic society; and they open a discussion about the impact of the advent of Islam on the status of women, a prominent topic in the contemporary Muslim world. The short *surahs* at the end of the Qur'an, the first to be revealed when Muhammad lived in Mecca, exemplify the moral thrust of Muhammad's early preaching and the Islamic conception of God's unity and power.

The Penguin translation of the Qur'an is problematic but relatively accessible for beginners. Ahmed Ali's *The Quran: A Contemporary Translation* reflects a modernist Islamic understanding. It has a parallel Arabic text, which helps make the point that Muslims do not regard any translation of the Qur'an as a true rendition of the word of God. A. J. Arberry's *The Koran Interpreted* emulates the style and spirit of the original Arabic, though it is the most difficult of these translations for beginning students. For background reading, W. Montgomery Watt's *Muhammad: Prophet and Statesman* is a solid biography of Muhammad from a traditional scholarly perspective sympathetic to Islam. Its argument has been sharply (but not entirely convincingly) challenged by the revisionist work of Patricia Crone, *Meccan Trade and the Rise of Islam,* and by Michael Cook, *Hagarism.* Michael Cook's *Muhammad,* a volume in the Past Masters series, is conveniently brief.

Contrary to the argument of the Pirenne thesis, the rise of Islam did not close the Mediterranean. Rather, the Arab conquests created what may be considered an Islamic common market. Starting in the mid-eighth century and peaking in the period of Fatimid rule in Egypt (969–1171), Muslim merchants established their dominance in Mediterranean commerce, and Islam became the hegemonic culture uniting both shores of the Mediterranean, as Rome did in antiquity. Gold Fatimid dinars circulated in a region delimited by Spain, Scandinavia, Muscovy, India, and China—a virtual "dollar of the Middle Ages." The mercantile ethos and social diversity of Fatimid Egypt is exemplified by the career of Ya`qub ibn Killis (d. 991)—a Jewish merchant born in Baghdad and a convert to Islam who was one of the architects of the Fatimid empire based in Cairo, where the new rulers established the first university in the Mediterranean basin, al-Azhar.

Islamic commercial expansion was accompanied by an agricultural revolution. According to Andrew Watson's *Agricultural Innovation in the Early Islamic World,* Muslims introduced at least seventeen new plant varieties into the Mediterranean region including rice, sugarcane, cotton, watermelons, eggplants, spinach, artichokes, sour oranges, lemons, limes, bananas, mangoes, and coconut palms. Muslims also initiated new irrigation techniques that expanded agricultural productivity. A twelfth-century Arabic cookbook whose title can loosely be translated as *The Way to the Beloved* lists more than 500 exotic recipes for chicken. The description of medieval recipes in Claudia Roden's *A Book of Middle Eastern Food* makes an entertaining class room recitation.

It is difficult to find texts suitable for a survey course on economic topics like these. One strategy might be to assign selections from Alfred F. Havighurst, ed., *The Pirenne Thesis: Analysis, Criticism, Revision* and pose the question: Why did Pirenne have such a negative view of Islam? Part of the answer would certainly be the influence of traditionally hostile European perceptions, which can be traced to the era of the Crusades.

Comparing Muslim and European experiences of the Crusades is an excellent exercise for which there are many suitable texts and a reasonable secondary literature. Excerpts from Arabic chronicles translated and edited by Francisco Gabrieli in *Arab Historians of the Crusades* convey the Muslim sense of cultural superiority. The selections on the Crusaders' massacre of the Muslims and Jews of Jerusalem (from the chronicle of Ibn al-Athir) and on Frankish medicine and Orientalized Franks (from the autobiography of Usama Ibn Munqidh) are particularly graphic. Amin Maalouf's, *The Crusades Through Arab Eyes* is a modern synthetic discussion of this issue. The Crusaders never occupied a major Muslim capital; they were eventually expelled and a strong Muslim state was reconstituted by Saladin. So from the Muslim point of view the Crusades were a minor and temporary military problem in a peripheral territory. However, historians whose project is the rise of the West often view the Crusades as the period when the balance of naval power between Islam and Christian Europe began to shift. After the year 1000 the commercial power of the Italian cities, which was enhanced by alliances with the Fatimids and their successors as well as by transporting and provisioning the Crusaders, gradually replaced the preeminent position of Muslim merchants in the Mediterranean.

The experiences of the Crusades and the Spanish Reconquista are reflected in several texts of the European literary canon that reveal interesting variations in their images of Islam. *The Song of Roland,* composed about the time of the first Crusade, can be read as a form of anti-Muslim war propaganda. The narrative is based on the Battle of Roncesvals (778) in which the Christian Gascons engaged the forces of Charlemagne; but in the poem the Gascons have been replaced by Muslims. *Roland* has an extremely hostile and ignorant view of Islam, regarding Muslims as heretics who worship a satanic trinity composed of Muhammad, Apollo, and Termagent. In contrast, *The Poem of the Cid* set during the Spanish Reconquista has a relatively benign and respectful view of Islam reflecting the fruitful coexistence of Muslims, Christians, and Jews in Spain during the Convivencia period. Dante's *Divine Comedy* was influenced by Arabic literary forms that entered Italy via Sicily. The *Inferno* contains a very harsh description of Muhammad as a sower of discord and heresy. But Dante is more appreciative of Averroes (Ibn Rushd in Arabic), who is included among the "noble pagans" in recognition of his contributions to Latin Christian culture.

Ibn Rushd (1126–98) is arguably the leading figure in the Arabo-Muslim philosophical and scientific tradition, which served as the transmission belt for the reintroduction of Greek thought into western Europe. In 800 the Caliph Harun al-Rashid established a teaching hospital in Baghdad, an enterprise that encouraged the extensive translation of Greek medical texts into Arabic. The first such translations were made by Masrjawayh, an Arabic-speaking Jew from Basra, around 720. Harun's successor, al-Ma'mun, established an academy (*Bayt al-Hikmah,* or House of Wisdom) and encouraged his court physician Hunayn ibn Ishaq (809–73) to translate Greek medical, philosophical, and scientific works. Hunayn systemized a method of translating from Greek to Arabic via Syriac and supervised the translation of works by Galen, Hippocrates, Plato, Aristotle, Euclid, and Archimedes. Others who flourished in the *Bayt al-Hikmah* include al-Khwarizmi (Algorismus in Latin, 780–850), who introduced the use of zero into Arab mathematics and founded the science of algebra.

The cultural disparity between the lands of Islam and Europe in this period is captured in Philip K. Hitti's pithy comment: "While al-Rashid and al-Ma'mun were delving into Greek and Persian philosophy their contemporaries in the West, Charlemagne and his lords, were reportedly dabbling in the art of writing their names" (*The Arabs: A Short History,* 2nd ed. Regnery Gateway, 1966, p. 120). This may not be entirely fair, because according to Einhard's biography Charlemagne knew Latin and some Greek, though he never did master writing his name.

Arabo-Islamic medical science, which developed Greek theory and practice, was also far more advanced than European medicine. Abu Bakr al-Razi (Rhazes in Latin, 865–925), the chief physician at the Baghdad hospital, composed a comprehensive medical encyclopedia (*al-Hawi,* or *Continens*) that was translated into Latin in 1279 by a Sicilian Jew, Faraj ibn Salim. Works by al-Razi and Ibn Sina (Avicenna in Latin, 980–1037) dominated the teaching of medicine in Europe until the end of the sixteenth century.

Al-Farabi (d. 950) and Ibn Sina developed ideas derived from Plotinus (d. 270), an Egyptian whose neo-Platonic synthesis became the best known version of the thought of Plato and Aristotle for Muslims until Ibn Rushd corrected many misinterpretations. Ibn Rushd, known as "the commentator," was the most important interpreter of Aristotle between late antiquity and the scholastics. Thomas Aquinas (1226–74) and the scholastics discovered Aristotle and Greek philosophy by reading translations from Arabic into Latin made by Jewish scholars living in Toledo after the Christian reconquest in 1085. Ralph Lerner and Muhsin Mahdi's edited volume, *Medieval Political Philosophy* contains selections from al-Farabi, Ibn Sina, Ibn Rushd and Aquinas as well as the Jewish scholar Maimonides (Moshe ben Maymon, 1135–1204), whose philosophical works written in Arabic use Aristotelian categories. Their common intellectual project consisted of an attempt to reconcile the Abrahamic and Socratic intellectual traditions by demonstrating that there was no contradiction between truths derived from reason and divine revelation. Majid al-Fakhry's *A History of Islamic Philosophy* provides a good overview of this topic.

Al-Ghazali (Algazel in Latin, 1058–1111) is commonly considered the synthesizer of the classical Islamic outlook. His intellectual autobiography, *Deliverance from Error* (translated by Montgomery Watt as *The Faith and Practice of al-Ghazali;* excerpted in William McNeill and Marilyn Robinson Waldman, eds., *The Islamic World*) considers scholastic theology, philosophy, shi`a theosophy, and mysticism (sufism) as alternative paths to truth. Although he was familiar with the Greek philosophical tradition as it had passed into Islam, al-Ghazali polemicized against it in *The Incoherence of the Philosophers.* Al-Ghazali sharply limited the scope of reason, concluding that a combination of *shari`a*-minded traditionalism and sufism constitute the surest path. *Deliverance from Error* is comparable to Augustine's *Confessions,* as both represent a departure from the Socratic tradition, which accorded primacy to human reason.

Ibn Khaldun (1332–1406) is the last great figure of medieval Arabo-Islamic philosophy. His *Muqaddimah* (*Prolegomena to History*) elaborates a philosophy of history and a theory of the state using materialist categories, although Ibn Khaldun undoubtedly considered himself a believing Muslim. *The Muqaddimah* has often been compared to Machiavelli's *The Prince*, as both discuss the real behavior of states and rulers in terms of historical processes independent of religious or moral norms. The abridgement of Franz Rosenthal's translation of *The Muqaddimah* is convenient to use.

With the expulsion of Jews and Muslims from Spain in 1492 and the shift of the dynamic center of Europe to the Atlantic northwest, it becomes more difficult to speak of a creative interaction between Islamic and Christian culture, but the conflict between the two societies continued to have a profound impact on the development of Europe. The Ottoman Empire remained a major power within the European state system until the late seventeenth century; and the Ottoman-Hapsburg rivalry was a significant factor contributing to the legal toleration of German Protestantism. Martin Luther originally regarded the Ottoman threat as a punishment for the sins of Christian Europe, and he viewed the Catholic Church as a greater enemy than the Ottomans. As the Ottomans were advancing on Vienna in 1529, Luther altered his views and advocated German unity against the Turks ("On War with the Turks"). Subsequently, the Protestant German princes of the Schmalkaldic League conditioned their participation in the defense of Vienna on obtaining religious toleration; and this was one of the factors that led Holy Roman Emperor Charles V to recognize Lutheranism in 1555.

In the modern era, the Middle East is part of the story of the expansion of the world capitalist market centered in Europe, of colonial settlement, and of imperial conquest. The French conquest of Algeria (1830), the construction of the Suez Canal (1869), the British occupation of Egypt (1882) and the conflicting British promises to the Arabs and Zionists during World War I are among the critical moments that have shaped the relationship between the Middle East and the West in the twentieth century. Frantz Fanon's *The Wretched of the Earth,* a product of the Algerian war of independence (1954–62), captures the anger and rejection of the West common to many Arabs and other formerly colonized peoples as they began to search for a new cultural and political orientation, while its central object of analysis—the emergent nation-states of the third world—is a product of Western influence.

A minimum program for integrating these topics into existing survey courses might focus on adding texts whose themes are comparable to texts often included in Western or world civilization courses. In that case selections from the Qur'an, from al-Ghazali's *Deliverance From Error,* and from Ibn Khaldun's *Muqaddimah* can be chosen. This strategy can justifiably be criticized as tokenism, as it introduces only a few texts and themes out of their original context primarily because of their relationship to the canonical themes of Western civilization. But it opens the door to viewing Arabo-Islamic culture as something not inherently hostile or foreign to the tradition many Americans claim as their own. This is, in my view, potentially a sufficient good to justify this practice.

A more ambitious and intellectually satisfying program would integrate many of the themes and texts discussed here into a traditional

Western civilization syllabus. Such a course is difficult to teach and demanding of students. But it can be done, and it offers many rewards.

Elements of this essay are a commentary on the syllabus of a one-year course designed by a group of Stanford faculty entitled Conflict and Change in Western Culture. That course simultaneously satisfied the requirements of the old Western Culture Program and pointed to the need for the reform, which was subsequently adopted. (Stanford's freshman humanities requirement has gone through two more revisions since then for reasons too complicated and contentious to review here.) Working as a team allowed faculty whose fields as commonly constructed might not intersect to transcend the limits of traditional disciplinary and interpretive categories. Involving literary scholars and sociologists as well as historians in teaching the course led us to prefer addressing broad themes over presenting a seamless historical narrative. Organizing the course around texts with comparable themes and using some less well-known texts allowed students to read and explicate them with a diminished sense of obligation to a received "correct" interpretation. Emphasizing the dynamic interaction and common elements of traditions commonly understood to be engaged in a confrontation rooted in an antagonism between the core values of their cultures encouraged some students to think more critically about popular images and definitions of issues related to the Middle East. These benefits more than compensated for the effort required to develop and teach a course of this nature.

Distant Neighbors:
Teaching about the Caribbean

Colin A. Palmer ◆ February 1995

Residents and nonresidents alike are exposed to a plethora of contrasting and conflicting representations of the Caribbean. The societies of the region are frequently depicted as exotic playgrounds with picturesque scenery, beautiful beaches, and smiling, congenial, and happy peoples. On occasion, these images are presented alongside those of unrelieved poverty, hopelessness, crime, and violence. Recently, the image includes that of drug-dependent societies held captive to a variety of crippling social ills and seemingly insoluble problems. But stereotypes aside, there are a variety of faces to these societies: they are richly diverse on the one hand, but there are deeply shared historic experiences and human and cultural ties on the other with which teachers of both United States and world history should be familiar.

The polyglot peoples of the Caribbean can trace their ancestry principally to Asia, Europe, and Africa. Few physical traces of the first inhabitants—the Guanahuatebys, Arawaks, and Caribs—remain. Almost all of the other contemporary residents can claim a history that began with the arrival of Christopher Columbus in the 1490s, and the extraordinary forces that were unleashed in the wake of European colonization. Today, the island societies and the enclaves on the South American mainland that are usually considered a part of the Caribbean have a combined population of approximately 35 million. Three states—Cuba, Haiti, and the Dominican Republic—account for about 70 percent of the total.

How should one teach about these societies? A relatively unscientific survey of the curricula of American universities indicates that there are at least five different kinds of courses that treat the Caribbean, either marginally or in substantial depth. The region is sometimes included as a part—albeit a small one—of world history surveys; it receives some attention in courses that address the history of the Americas; and thematic offerings on the history of the Atlantic slave trade, comparative slavery, social revolutions—among others— also draw examples from the region. A few universities offer survey or specialized courses whose primary focus is the history of the area, and there are courses with an interdisciplinary emphasis, usually containing historical segments but also devoting substantial attention to the literature, economy, social and cultural institutions, and political life of the peoples. This short discussion is primarily concerned with those courses in which the history of the Caribbean people receives more than just a superficial treatment, although others are likely to profit as well.

The matter of how to define the Caribbean invites attention from the outset. Should the criteria be primarily geographic, cultural, or based upon some other measure? The answer to this question will depend on whether one accepts the view that the societies washed by the Caribbean Sea possess a cultural unity that tempers their individual trajectories or whether one chooses to see each society as fundamentally unique in its historical evolution and contemporary character.

Recently I attended a workshop in Miami where a few scholars maintained that South Florida should now be considered a part of the Caribbean because of the significant presence and cultural impact of Jamaicans, Puerto Ricans, Haitians, Cubans, and others. In this rendering, the Caribbean consists of moving frontiers, the geographically disparate societies are united by shared cultural understandings. Other scholars would include Venezuela, Panama, Costa Rica, and the Yucatán because of the long history of cultural interaction and exchange between these peoples and others linked by the Caribbean Sea. Scholars may divide on the boundaries of the Caribbean and the criteria for establishing them, but the issue must be addressed and the reasons for the inclusion or exclusion of some societies must withstand informed analysis.

History courses that discuss the Caribbean, regardless of how the area is defined, can no longer start in 1492 with the arrival of Columbus; such a perspective is not only Eurocentric but ahistorical as well. Significant attention must be given to the internal history of the first inhabitants of the area, their system of thought, economic arrangements, and the ways in which they organized their lives prior to the fateful events of 1492. Our students must develop a balanced and healthy appreciation of those diverse societies, shorn of the ethnocentrism or romantic condescension that has often interfered with our study of the early peoples of the Americas. They must be able to situate the indigenous peoples in their own cultural and geographic space and seek to understand them in their own context. Moreover, it is important not to define these ethnically variegated people by the appellation "pre-Hispanic" because such a description tends to see them as important only in terms to their relationship to the European "Other."

The events of 1492 present special interpretive problems. We cannot characterize the European arrival as a "discovery," given the Eurocentric connotations of that word when used in this context. But did this historically momentous occurrence and its aftermath constitute a "conquest," an "invasion," a "collision," or merely an "encounter"? This is more than just a semantic problem. Our characterization of the nature of those events will shape in large measure how we—and our students too—interpret subsequent developments and the relationships between the outsiders and the indigenous people.

The imposition of European rule after 1492 was an important watershed in the history of the Caribbean. But while we cannot and should not deny the fundamental changes that European colonial rule wrought, it is important to search for watersheds in the evolution of the indigenous peoples prior to 1492. In other words, the tendency to view these early societies as static must be avoided. The rise of sedentary communities, for example, represented an important break with past practices and understandings, and so did the development of agriculture. These and other innovations occurred at different times in different places but they presaged new societal challenges and directions.

Post-1492 watersheds, to be sure, are easy to identify if for no other reason than the historical literature is more abundant. In addition to the inauguration of colonial rule, the demographic consequences of the European presence were catastrophic for the local peoples. These related developments, together with the introduction of African slavery in 1502, must be seen as important benchmarks in the history of the area. Most of the islands, with notable exceptions such as Cuba and

Puerto Rico, had majority black populations by 1700 and maturing plantation economies, with enormous consequences for their racial, cultural, and economic configurations.

The achievement of emancipation at various times in the nineteenth century must also be viewed as representing sharp breaks in the old regimen, as did the social and political movements of the 1930s and 1940s. The Cuban Revolution and the achievement of political independence by some countries in the 1960s and later should also be seen as initiating, or at least as having the potential to chart, new directions in their societal orders. Historians of the region may properly disagree with the identification and timing of these watersheds and with the measure of their significance. The point I wish to emphasize, however, is that the watersheds that are identified must be rooted in the internal history of the peoples of the region, be centered in their experiences, and reflect their own struggles and achievements.

As a practical matter, post-1492 developments will undoubtedly constitute the major emphases of most courses. The literature is more extensive, as I have noted, and there is a host of complex issues to be analyzed. Because African slavery was established in 1502 and racism became systemic in all of the societies, a credible course on the Caribbean—as well as on any that brings the region into focus—can hardly avoid a discussion of the ideological bases of racial slavery and the roles that "race" as an independent agency played and continues to play.

Students in our classes must appreciate the fact that there was nothing inevitable about the introduction of African slaves in the Caribbean or elsewhere in this hemisphere. It was only one of several labor options Europeans confronted. Some historians have, unwittingly, come dangerously close to embracing the view that the enslavement of Africans was not only inevitable but indispensable for the successful colonization of the Americas by the Europeans. We must be certain that our students develop some understanding of the complex roots of racial slavery and its ideological, cultural, and economic matrices.

The process by which the Caribbean was colonized and the nature of the colonial regimes and societies deserve attention. The colonial powers established the legal boundaries within which the free and enslaved operated, and they promoted an ideology that legitimized the social order. We cannot, of course, revert to the practice of earlier times when the real stuff of Caribbean history consisted almost entirely of the activities of the colonizers, their competition for new possessions, and the wars they fought in the area. These issues, to be sure, are not unimportant and so must form part of the story; rather, it is largely a matter of perspective and balance. The history of the emerging black majorities in most islands should, I would suggest, be the principal—but not the exclusive—focus of our attention. In time, they would give these societies their distinctive identities and shape their social, cultural, and political trajectories.

Fortunately, historians can no longer lament the paucity of literature on the Atlantic slave trade and slavery. The last two decades have witnessed a veritable flood of scholarly work in this area, much of it reflecting a commendable methodological sophistication. Studies of the slave trade by Philip Curtin, *The Atlantic Slave Trade: A Census;* Herbert Klein, *The Middle Passage: Comparative Studies in the Atlantic Slave Trade;* James Rawley, *The Transatlantic Slave Trade: A History;* David Galenson, *Traders, Planters, and Slaves: Market Behavior in Early English America;* Robert Louis Stein, *The French Slave Trade in the Eighteenth Century: An Old Regime Business;* and Johannes Menne Postma, *The Dutch in the Atlantic Slave Trade, 1600–1815* have shed considerable light on its changing organizational structure, the ethnic origins or the human cargoes, the process of their enslavement, the nature of the Atlantic passage, and a variety of demographic issues. This new information must be incorporated into our discussions of the Caribbean, but the slave trade cannot be seen as merely the movement of peoples. Africa—in all of its cultural richness and diversity—came to the Caribbean and to the Americas as a whole, as Michael Mullin has argued in *Africa in America: Slave Acculturation and Resistance in the American South and the Caribbean, 1736–1831.* Consequently, our students must obtain a deep understanding of the various ethnic streams and cultures that went into the making of the Caribbean.

The experiences of the slaves in the different societies at particular times remains controversial and imperfectly understood. Justice cannot be done to these debates here. Suffice it to say that our students should not view the history of these enslaved persons through the masters' lens or see them principally as helpless victims, emotionally drained, and socially dead. The tendency—at the other extreme—to characterize slaves as being always on the barricades and existing in a permanent state of rage represents a caricature of their lives, complex inner storms, and physical struggles. There is no doubt, of course, that African-born slaves and their Creole progeny struggled to maintain a healthy sense of self and their psychic balance, even as they created the institutions that would sustain them as a people.

A good deal of the recent literature on slavery in the Caribbean and other societies of the Americas has avoided any discussion of the brutality of the institution and its impact on its victims and those who exercised power over them. Although this is an area of inquiry fraught with all kinds of minefields, we should question whether slaves, in teflon-coated fashion, walked away from their awful experiences unscathed. In fact, to suggest that slavery had a deleterious impact on its victims and their owners is, fundamentally, to affirm their common humanity. What must remain uncertain, and contentious, is the degree of that impact, its nature, and extent.

In exploring, or at least acknowledging, this controversial and emotionally charged issue, we must make a theoretical distinction between the impact of slavery on the enslaved, on the one hand, and the culture, social institutions, and sustaining mechanisms they created, on the other. The two questions are different but they are also interrelated. The distinction between the two is often blurred in some of the literature, resulting in seriously flawed portraits of the institution of slavery and an overly "feel good" celebration of "slave" culture. The enslaved paid an enormous physical and psychic price as human property, and the circumstances that shaped the development of their culture—as important and exuberant as that was—should not be minimized.

Having said this, I think it is also desirable to devote considerable attention in our courses to the worlds of work, to the ways in which the enslaved ordered their lives, belief systems, worldviews, medical practices, internal economies, and to the range of responses—from accommodation to resistance—to their life situations. It is important, wherever possible, to explore the degree of social stratification within the slave community and to make distinctions between the African-born and the Creoles as they coped with their realities. All too frequently, we see the enslaved as a homogeneous group of people, bereft of any individuality. Slavery as an institution was never static, and the reactions of its victims were neither unchanging, uniform, nor predictable. An underlying and pervasive theme in our discussions of slavery should be the process by which the Caribbean became culturally Africanized.

The emancipation of the slaves at various times in the nineteenth century brought new challenges and possibilities. In fact, the ways in which the newly freed organized their lives and attempted to shape their futures and create a livable space for themselves constituted the principal themes of postemancipation history. The process and meanings of freedom varied and so did the responses to the changing circumstances, as Rebecca Scott has shown in her *Slave Emancipation in Cuba: The Transition to Free Labor, 1860–1889* and Thomas Holt in *The Problem of Freedom: Race, Labor, and Politics in Jamaica and Britain, 1832–1938*. The arrival of the East Indians and the Chinese as indentured servants in some societies underscored an acute shortage of plantation workers, simultaneously adding new cultural and ethnic streams to the host societies.

The task of making sense of internal developments in the nineteenth century and later is complicated by the need to recognize the interplay between local forces and the ubiquitous external actors. Caribbean societies, probably because of their size, have seldom been free from external interference and control. The Cuban struggle for independence, for example, was stymied by the imposition of the Platt Amendment. Puerto Rico was virtually absorbed by the United States after the Spanish-Cuban-American war. And Haiti, the Dominican Republic, and Grenada have been invaded by American troops in more recent times. The role of the former Soviet Union in the affairs of Cuba is another striking example of external influence. The penetration of foreign capital, political ideas, and culture have also had enormous consequences for almost all of the societies and can and should be examined most usefully in a comparative context.

But while the Caribbean area has been subjected to foreign influences of one sort or another, this has never been a one-sided affair; migration is a dominant theme in the history of the region, particularly in the twentieth century. England, the United States, Central America, and Canada, for example, have been the destinations of a considerable number of the area's residents. Similarly, refugees from the great slave revolution in Haiti left their cultural imprint on Louisiana and elsewhere, as Alfred Hunt has recently shown in his *Haiti's Influence on Antebellum America*. The Jamaican Marcus Garvey organized a mass movement in the United States in the early decades of the twentieth century, and the ideology of an aggressive and confident blackness that inspired it still has a profound resonance in black America.

External influence and migration aside, the twentieth-century Caribbean invites analysis from a variety of other perspectives. The social movements that challenged the status quo in so many societies in the 1930s and later reflected the emergence of a new social order. The labor unrest that became almost endemic in those decades was symptomatic of deeper societal tensions and presaged bitter struggles for social justice and political rights. The configuration of these battles was, understandably, shaped by the circumstances of each society. In the case of the British West Indies, there were demands for universal adult suffrage, internal self-government, and, ultimately, political independence. Cuba, on the other hand, experienced a social revolution and asserted its independence from the United States. A profound sense of nationalism gave life to these struggles while simultaneously legitimizing them.

The political leaders who have emerged since the 1930s have confronted distressingly similar problems, although their prescriptions for change have been diverse. The states of the region are uniformly poor, and the structural barriers to reform have been remarkably resilient. The Cuban Revolution represented one model for change, while the democratic socialism of Jamaica's Michael Manley seemed to suggest another. Puerto Rico tied its fortunes to the United States, and a series of rapacious and dictatorial administrations in Haiti

ignored the problems of the dispossessed. With few remaining exceptions, Caribbean societies have won their political independence, and
they share many of the same problems that have bedeviled the
nations of Africa, Asia, and Latin America. Some of these historical
issues can be explored from a comparative perspective, an approach
that will certainly temper any tendency to paint a picture of Caribbean
exceptionalism.

Inasmuch as we must give voice to the dispossessed in our teaching of the history of the area, we should be similarly sensitive to the role
that gender has played in helping to determine an individual's life
chances. Specialists in the field have recently begun to employ gender
as a mode of analysis, a methodological development that is certain to
transform our understanding of the evolution of these societies.
Similarly, the experiences of women must be included in the story that
is being told, altering it in the process. Recent contributions by Hilary
Beckles, *Natural Rebels: A Social History of the Enslaved Black Women
in Barbados, 1627–1838;* Marietta Morrissey, *Slave Women in the New
World: Gender Stratification in the Caribbean;* and Barbara Bush, *Slave
Women in Caribbean Society, 1690–1838* have enlarged our understanding of the lives of enslaved women, but such studies are still in
their infancy. The complex interplay of race, class, and gender in cir-
cumscribing an individual's or a group's possibilities is a characteristic
of all the societies.

This brief discussion does not exhaust the principal themes that
should inform any discussion of the history of the Caribbean. An
inescapable and continuing challenge is to present a picture that under-
scores the underlying cultural and historical unity of the area, while not
losing sight of its diversity. A dynamic balance, therefore, must be struck
between our recognition of the regional commonalties on the one hand
and of the unique historical trajectory of each society on the other. We
must, in other words, eschew any tendency to homogenize the experiences of these societies or to exaggerate their heterogeneity.

The recounting of the history of these people should not be trivi-
alized and reduced exclusively to simplistic, patronizing, and mecha-
nized discussions of the physical resistance of slaves or of the
contemporary poor to their unenviable condition. Nor should we
depict their history solely in terms of a tough, resilient people who
have not been affected adversely, if at all, by the roll of history's
unlucky dice. Their story is much more multifaceted, complex, and
textured than such all-too-popular renderings suggest. In the end, the
history of the Caribbean, like the history of any other people, must be
told—in large measure—from the perspective of those who made it
and lived it. The interplay between the internal realities and the external forces must be given weight, but it is the Caribbean people

themselves—with all their human strengths and vulnerabilities—who must occupy center stage as we seek to understand their experiences. Avoiding both hagiography and the temptation to view these peoples as the broken victims of malevolent forces, we are compelled to reconstruct their past, and to write and teach their history with empathy, a critical eye, and respect.

Joining the Mainstream: Integrating Latin America into the Teaching of World History

William F. Sater ◆ May/June 1995

After countless hours of labor, I have concluded that it appears almost foolhardy to try to cram all of Latin America into a world history course. The term Latin America is itself a misnomer: the area extending south from the Rio Grande to Tierra del Fuego derives only a portion of its culture from the Iberian nations. And while many people speak either Spanish or, in Brazil, Portuguese, large numbers still use a variety of Indian languages, including Quechua, Aymara, and Nahuatl. In short, the nations of Latin America may occupy the same continent, but significant racial and cultural differences distinguish them. Talking about Latin America is about as accurate as talking about Europe, which, although smaller in size and population, continues to be considered more diverse than other regions of the world. Thus, rather than utilizing geopolitical terms, teachers might divide Latin America into four racial blocs: the largely Indian nations of Bolivia, Peru, Paraguay, and Ecuador; the mestizo countries like Mexico, Chile, El Salvador, and Colombia; states with large black or mulatto components, such as Brazil and some Caribbean islands; and the predominately white societies of Uruguay and Argentina. This way, instructors could acknowledge Latin America's diverse population while still integrating it into world history courses.

CONQUEST AND SETTLEMENT

What makes Latin America unique is that the European nations not only integrated it economically, but legally incorporated it into their royal patrimonies. To understand this process, particularly the role of the state and the individual explorers, teachers should study the Spanish *Reconquista* as well as the pre-Colombian Indians. Various authors give some insight into the three most populous Indian cultures—the Aztecs, Mayas, and Incas—as well as those of Brazil, which were neither as large nor perhaps as culturally advanced as those of Mexico and the

Pacific side of South America.[1] Because the European presence—race, language, religion, and culture—is more deeply imprinted in the Western Hemisphere, Latin America shares more in common with the United States than with Asia or Africa where colonists arrived later and where the impact does seem not as permanent. Spain and Portugal, after all, controlled portions of North and all of Central and South America for approximately 300 years.

Students might benefit from reading some of the European accounts of the conquest and settlement of Mexico, Peru, or other parts of what became Spain and Portugal's empires. Although the explorers who came to these areas may have caused great destruction, the experiences of these audacious *conquistadores* certainly constitute one of the great human adventures. Students, for example, could compare the exultant letters of Cortés or Bernal Diaz, describing their exploits, with the experiences of those who settled the United States, Canada, and Africa or Asia. Teachers can also use recent scholarship that documents the less than enthusiastic Indian response toward those Europeans who seized their lands and who, in some cases, literally eradicated their culture.

The conquest of the Western Hemisphere changed both Latin America and Europe. In exchange for the potato, tomato, corn, and precious metals, Latin America received European religion, technology, languages, and culture. Perhaps the most important initial European contribution was disease: not merely smallpox and tuberculosis, which also annihilated the Europeans, but also the presumably more benign ailments of influenza, measles, mumps, and chicken pox. Without any natural immunities and often abused or ill fed, the Amerindian population perished by the millions. Teachers might compare the devastating demographic impact of the smallpox pandemic, which annihilated up to 90 percent of the Amerindian population, with the effect of European exploration on Africa or Asia. Disease traveled both ways across the Atlantic: just as malaria devastated European settlers in Africa, the Americas retaliated by giving their unwelcome guests syphilis.

Some Europeans migrated to Spanish and Portuguese America, as they did to England's American colonies, but not in sufficient numbers to compensate for the loss of native life. How the Europeans coped with labor shortages is yet another interesting topic. Early in the sixteenth century, Spanish colonists created first the *repartamiento* and then the *encomienda,* institutions that recruited and allocated Indian labor to till the fields and work the mines.[2] When the local population succumbed either to disease or abuse, Europeans first supplemented and then replaced the Indians with other Indians or with slaves from Africa. Again, this process seems to have occurred on a larger scale in Latin America than in British America or the rest of the world.

Slavery, moreover, permeated all of Latin America, although later the slaves tended to be concentrated more heavily in areas that produced valuable agricultural products or minerals where their labor was most needed. In some countries, such as Chile, the black population slowly disappeared through the process of miscegenation; in others, like Brazil, which did not abolish slavery until the end of the nineteenth century, blacks constituted a significant portion of the population. Teachers could compare the Latin American slave trade with the transfer of blacks across the North Atlantic, the Indian Ocean, the Mediterranean, as well as their movement within Africa. Additionally, there are various examples of indentured servitude. Many of the Spanish came to the Americas as indentured laborers, which can be contrasted with the experience of contract labor in the United States or the British Empire.

Christianity, particularly the Roman Catholic Church, remains one of the most enduring of the European legacies to Latin America, as it is to the United States. While the church transferred pernicious institutions like the Inquisition to the Americas, it also provided most of the culture that existed in the colonies. Religious communities, moreover, operated orphanages, hospitals, foundling homes, schools, and universities. Religious holidays became social occasions. The Latin American Church ministered to the pocketbook as well as the soul. Over the decades, the church accumulated land that it sometimes organized into *haciendas*. It also received tithes and donations, which it lent out to those in need of capital. While clearly tied to the elites, it was the church, as an arm of the Spanish state, that afforded the Indians the little protection they received. Bartolome de las Casas and others defended Indian rights in the Spanish court; the regular orders, the Franciscans, Dominicans, Augustinians, and Jesuits, charged with converting the Indians, tried to protect their charges from the rapacious European settlers.

Although lacking the current allure of social history, economic topics present the classroom instructor with a particularly useful area for exposition. Latin America provided more resources to Europe, and for a longer period of time, than Asia, Africa, or what became the United States. Peruvian and Mexican gold and particularly silver funded Spain for decades. While not as lucrative, cultivating the land provided its owner with some wealth and more prestige. The new colonial masters created agricultural units—called, depending on the region, *haciendas, fundos, estancias, fazendas*—that produced commercially important crops like sugar or pastoral products, such as meat, hides, and tallow; other units raised horses and mules for commercial use. Happily, teachers can easily obtain information not merely on the evolution of the *hacienda* economy, but also on specific estates, some of which were enormous, almost self-sufficient economic entities. The development of a plantation system can be contrasted with a similar process in the United States, Africa, or Asia, which also raised raw materials for export. In addition, there were smaller farms, the *ranchos,* as well as self-sufficient Indian communities, which evolved into an important component of the colonial economy. These agricultural units generally began to satisfy the needs of nearby urban administrative or mining centers and slowly started to export their produce to other portions of the empire and, eventually, to Spain or Portugal. Finally, local industries and artisanal workshops manufactured consumer goods, like textiles or shoes, and prepared foods for local markets as well as for other colonies. The traffic in the produce of the mines, *haciendas,* and factories spawned a network of commercial houses that acted as intermediaries both within the Americas and between the colonies and Europe. More than the English or the Portuguese, the Spanish developed cities that, as the economy grew, became a source of employment for administrators and service industries. Teachers certainly could compare the Latin American process of urbanization to the growth of cities in Asia, Africa, and the United States.

Thanks to the expansion of the economy, the establishment of imperial government bodies, the introduction of the military, and the presence of the church, colonial Latin America developed a complicated social structure. Two forces shaped the colonial society: traditional European values, which tended to favor the nobility, the military, and the clergy over commerce and, of course, the peasants; and a new component: race. Certainly Latin America's racial mix was more varied than that of Europe, British America, Africa, or Asia. From the intermingling of the Amerindian, the European, and later the black and Asian, came the fruits of miscegenation—the *mestizo,* mulatto, *zambo,* and *chino.* If race played an important part in determining status—many felt the need to prove their *limpieza de sangre* (that their blood was untainted by inferior people)—wealth and education could also affect one's social standing. Teachers could compare how Latin America's racial minorities absorbed European values to advance socially and economically with the same process of acculturation in Africa and Asia.

Invariably, teachers should dedicate some material to studying the political development of the Iberian colonies. It might prove more useful to concentrate on the larger nations—Mexico, Peru, or Brazil—about which much has been written, rather than try to include every part of the empire.[3] While this selection process excludes the smaller countries, it provides one of the few ways to cover the material in an efficient manner. Teachers can supplement political history with material on blacks or Asians in the workforce, compare Latin American religious dissidents to those in the United States, and contrast the somewhat privileged legal and economic status of colonial Latin American women with their sisters across the oceans.[4]

INDEPENDENCE

After the United States, the nations of Latin America became some of the first former colonial possessions to become free. After centuries of putative imperial domination, Luso-Hispanic Americans developed a sense of identity that distinguished, and later alienated, them from their European rulers. Spain's eighteenth-century attempts to reassert its control over its dominions antagonized the local elites who, over the decades, had wielded substantial economic, political, and social power. The American upper class and masses objected, sometimes violently, to the Spanish crown's policies. Like the United States, Latin America initially sought not so much independence but more local autonomy. The Napoleonic Wars, however, so diminished the Iberian nations' strength that Latin America's elites could displace their colonial masters. Depending on the area, however, this process of emancipation occurred over decades before the rebels drove Spanish forces from the mainland.

The independence process was complex and essentially there were two phases: a political revolution in the Spanish world and the breakup of the Spanish monarchy. The process varied from country to country. Some nations fought for it; others had independence thrust upon them. Because Madrid often utilized locally recruited militias, the wars for independence became more civil struggles than movements for national liberation. This became particularly true as Latin American elites battled the masses who attempted to use the political unrest to obtain redress for their social and economic problems. A few nations, like Brazil, achieved independence in a relatively bloodless process and long after many other nations had won their freedom. Many of the Caribbean islands remained colonial possessions. Certainly students could profit from comparing the Latin American struggle for freedom, which, like that of the United States, required prolonged fighting, with that of Asia and Africa.[5]

Given this chaotic political process, independence may have brought freedom but it did not confer stability. The oligarchy continued to wage a war on the masses and to fight each other. For many years the ever-exotic Brazil remained the continent's only monarchy. Ideological conflicts roiled the hemisphere, and while they sometimes shared general themes—arguments over the type of government, federalism versus centralism, the status of the church, guarantees of individual rights—each nation's search for a solution appeared unique. Some countries, like Chile, established authoritarian governments that slowly, and sometimes in response to violent protest from below, evolved into more liberal states. A few countries never, in fact, became polities. Under the sometimes benign influence of what are called *caudillos*, areas such as Bolivia and Paraguay fluttered between chaos and authoritarianism.

The Twentieth Century

Eventually change came to Latin America as it did to Europe and the United States: Argentina, Chile, and Uruguay voluntarily empowered their citizens, enfranchising first all men and then, by the mid-twentieth century, women. In some countries, foreign intervention or constant civil unrest aborted or slowed the political process. These countries appeared stuck in some political limbo, but eventually even they changed. Latin American nations, unlike those in Africa, Europe, or Asia, rarely became one-party states, nor have they, with the exception of Cuba, embraced the ideas of either political extreme. Brazil's *Estado Novo* or Chile's Socialist Republic (which, in fact, was neither) might have briefly espoused totalitarian ideals, but it was nationalism that emerged as the predominant ideology. Given the number of countries involved, a teacher would be best advised to concentrate on the hemisphere's largest nations—Argentina, Brazil, Chile, and Mexico, about which a great deal has been written—rather than to attempt some continental analysis on political development.[6]

The history of Latin America, like that of other areas, becomes a process of modifying traditional institutions. The abolition of slavery, for example, constitutes an important topic that a teacher can usefully compare with similar processes in the United States, Africa, and Asia.[7] Ending slavery did not undo the damage done to the black community, because the freed slaves remained subordinated to the dominant white oligarchy in places like Brazil as well as in the United States. Teachers can compare how Latin American nations dealt with this issue as well as that of race.

The unequal landholding system continued to plague Latin America just as it did other areas of the world. Agrarian reform sought to wrest control from the landholding minority and give it to the peons, who tilled the soil and whose conditions approximated those of serfs. In some countries, such as Mexico, people had to fight to bring justice to the countryside. Others accomplished similar changes peacefully. The secularization of society, which eventually led to the separation of church and state—sometimes preceded by the despoiling of the clergy—offers yet another subject for historical comparisons with nations where state support for religion seemed minimal. Diplomatic relations among independent states, their former colonial masters, and the rest of the world offers another fruitful area for exploration. Latin American nations, for example, often had difficulty winning the diplomatic recognition of Spain, a problem that did not bedevil the United States or many of the former Asian or African colonies, and that complicated their development. Latin America, moreover, had to deal with another colonial legacy: uncertain boundaries. For decades, frontier disputes, which occasionally blossomed into war, bedeviled the continent.

Finally, teachers might compare the experience of Latin America's women or minority or ethnic groups with those of the United States, Asia, and Africa. The struggle of Latin American women to become enfranchised as well as to regain many of the economic rights they possessed in the colonial period can be placed alongside the experience of women on other continents. Countless immigrants—Arabs, Germans, Italians, Chinese, Jews, and Japanese—poured into Argentina, Chile, Brazil, and Peru. Relating their stories would allow teachers to address the issues of assimilation, a topic that could be enhanced by including the experience of the black and the Amerindian.[8] Lately a new area of emphasis has appeared: the study of the so-called "muted classes", which notes how the peasants, contrary to popular beliefs, confronted the political process and the forces of modernization.[9]

Comparing the process of Latin America's modern economic development is a valuable adjunct to studying Latin American political evolution. Latin America's economies tended to adjust rapidly in response to world market conditions. Teachers can describe this process in a variety of ways. Some might attempt to trace economic change on a country-by-country basis. A better alternative is to emphasize specific economic examples rather than nations. For instance, students can learn about tropical economies by studying the production of sugar, coffee, or bananas in Brazil, Ecuador, Central America, or Peru. Some Latin American nations, such as Argentina, developed pastoral economies, exporting meat or cereals. As in the colonial period, the exploitation of mineral resources—the mining of copper, nitrates, silver, or guano in Chile, Mexico, and Peru, or the exploitation of oil in Mexico and Venezuela—proved more lucrative than tilling the ground above them.[10]

Relying on mines and fields tended to create monocultures that left Latin American producers, as it did their American, Asian, and African counterparts, at the mercy of the vagaries of world market demand. Industrialization occurred in Latin America, but not without difficulty. Latin American nations, like other nations, depended upon the customs house as their main source of income. Instituting protectionist laws, while helping nascent industries, deprived the new nations of needed revenues. By the late nineteenth century, however, countries like Chile, Argentina, and Mexico began to build tariff walls to shelter local manufacturers. These industries provided an alternative source of employment to agriculture or mining, completing the process of economic development.

The Great Depression constituted a watershed in Latin America as it did in the United States. Various countries accepted the notion that the state should foster economic development and eventually, depending upon the situation, ownership of or, at a minimum, control over subsoil resources. As in the rest of the world, government-sponsored import substitution became the vehicle in the drive for self-sufficiency and industrialization.[11]

The growth of population and economic development accelerated the process of urbanization and stimulated the formation of unions. The development of an industrial and entrepreneurial class altered Latin America's social system. Locally trained intellectuals staffed government bureaucracies, such as Chile's CORFO, where they helped shape economic policy. Again, comparing these institutions with others, such as the TVA, can illustrate the role of the state in fomenting economic development. Post-World War II immigration, first from Europe and then Asia, increased the continent's ethnic and racial diversity.

At the end of this brief essay, we return to the starting point: how can one teach about more than twenty diverse nations, let alone compare them to Asia, Africa, Europe, or the United States? As this essay indicates, there are many topics that can easily be included in a world history course. Teachers should take care to emphasize general trends rather than become involved in a specific nation's history. Certainly Latin America's rich past and diverse population provide instructors and students with ample material for comparison with other areas of the world.

NOTES

1. Frances Berdan, *The Aztecs of Central Mexico: An Imperial Society* (New York: Holt, Rinehart, and Winston, 1982) and John Hemming, *Red Gold: The Conquest of the Brazilian Indians* (Cambridge, Mass.: Harvard Univ. Press, 1978).

2. See Lesley Simpson's *The Encomienda. Forced Native Labor in the Spanish Colonies, 1492–1550* (Berkeley: Univ. of California Press, 1929) and *The Encomienda in New Spain* (Berkeley: Univ. of California Press, 1950).

3. General histories for the principal areas are Jaime Rodriguez and Colin Maclachlan, *The Forging of the Cosmic Race: A Reinterpretation of Colonial Mexico* (Berkeley: Univ. of California Press, 1990) or Dauril Alden, *Royal Government in Colonial Brazil* (Berkeley: Univ. of California Press, 1968).

4. Selected topics on colonial life should include a discussion on the status of various sectors. Leslie Rout Jr., *The African Experience in Spanish America, 1502 to the Present Day* (Cambridge: Cambridge Univ. Press, 1976) discusses the status of blacks. Asuncion Lavrín's *Latin American Women: Historical Perspectives* (Westport, Conn.: Greenwood Press, 1978) and her edited work, *Sexuality and Marriage in Colonial Latin America* (Lincoln: Univ. of Nebraska Press, 1992), and Patricia Seed, To *Love, Honor, and Obey in Colonial Mexico: Conflict over Marriage Choice, 1574–1821* (Stanford: Stanford Univ. Press, 1988), examine women's roles. S. Liebman, *New World Jewry* (New

York: Ktav Publishing House, 1982) traces the plight of the Jews.

5. Jaime Rodriguez, *The Independence of Spanish America* (Cambridge: Cambridge Univ. Press, 1998) provides an excellent study of the revolutionary process. Lester Langley, *The Americas in the Age of Revolution, 1750–1850* (New Haven, Conn.: Yale Univ. Press, 1998) compares the revolutionary process in the United States, Haiti, and Latin America.

6. For the various countries, see David Rock, *Argentina, 1516–1987* (Berkeley: Univ. of California Press, 1987); Ronald M. Schneider, *Order and Progress. A Political History of Brazil* (Boulder, Colo.: Westview Press, 1991); Arthur Whitaker, *The United States and the Southern Cone: Argentina, Chile, and Uruguay* (Cambridge, Mass.: Harvard Univ. Press, 1976); Simon Collier and William Sater, *The History of Chile* (Cambridge: Cambridge Univ. Press, 1996); Frederick Pike, *The United States and the Andean Republics* (Cambridge, Mass.: Harvard Univ. Press, 1977); and Michael Meyers and William Sherman, *The Course of Mexican History* (New York: Oxford Univ. Press, 1983).

7. A newer work, Joseph E. Harris et al., eds., *The African Diaspora* (College Station: Texas A&M Univ., Dept. of Anthropology, 1996) provides a series of articles that professors would find useful for comparative purposes. See also David Murray, *Odious Commerce: Britain, Spain and the Abolition of the Cuban Slave Trade* (Cambridge: Cambridge Univ. Press, 1980) and John Lombardi, *The Decline and Abolition of Negro Slavery in Venezuela* (Westport, Conn.: Greenwood Press, 1971). Predictably, the issue of slavery became more important in Brazil, which had imported more slaves and had the largest black population of any Latin American country. See L. Bethell, *The Abolition of the Brazilian Slave Trade* (Cambridge: Cambridge Univ. Press, 1970) and Robert Conrad, *The Destruction of Brazilian Slavery* (Berkeley: Univ. of California Press, 1972).

8. Examples are Julie Hahner, *Emancipating the Female Sex: The Struggle for Women's Rights in Brazil, 1850–1940* (Durham, N.C.: Duke Univ. Press, 1990); Marifan Carlson, *Feminismo! The Woman's Movement in Argentina from its Beginnings to Eva Peron* (Chicago: Univ. of Chicago Press, 1988); and Shirlene Soto, *Emergence of the Modern Mexican Woman: Her Participation in Revolution and Struggle for Equality, 1910–1940* (Denver: Arden Press, 1990). For an overview, see Sandra McGee Deutch, "Gender and Sociopolitical Change in Twentieth Century Latin America" *Hispanic American Historical Review* 71 (2): 259–306 (1991). For various ethnic and religious groups, see Frederick Luebke, *Germans in the New World* (Champaign: Univ. of Illinois Press, 1990); Ronald Newton, *German Buenos Aires* (Austin: Univ. of Texas Press, 1977); Judith L. Elkin and G. Merkx, *The Jewish Presence in Latin America* (Boston: Allen and Unwin, 1987); and Tim

Holloway, *Immigration on the Land* (Chapel Hill: Univ. of North Carolina Press, 1980). There are also materials on the immigration of Italians, Japanese, and even the Welsh.

9. See Peter Guardino, *Peasants, Politics, and the Formation of Mexico's National States: Guerreo, 1800–1857* (Stanford, Calif.: Stanford Univ. Press, 1996); Terry Rugeley, *Yucatan's Maya Peasantry and the Origins of the Caste War* (Austin: Univ. of Texas Press, 1996); and Paul Vanderwood, *The Power of God against the Guns of Government: Religious Upheaval in Mexico at the Turn of the Nineteenth Century* (Stanford, Calif.: Stanford Univ. Press, 1998).

10. For a discussion of Latin America's mining and agrarian endeavors, see, for Chile, Thomas O'Brien, *The Nitrate Industry and Chile's Critical Transition* (New York: New York Univ. Press, 1982). For coffee, see Mauricio Font, *Coffee, Contention, and Change in the Making of Modern Brazil* (Cambridge, Mass.: Harvard Univ. Press, 1990); Peter Eisenberg, *The Sugar Industry in Pernambunco* (Berkeley: Univ. of California Press, 1974); and M. Palacios, *Coffee in Colombia, 1870–1970* (Cambridge: Cambridge Univ. Press, 1980). For agriculture and pastoral issues, see James Scobie, *Revolution on the Pampa: A Social History of Argentine Wheat, 1860–1910* (Austin: Univ. of Texas Press, 1964) and Peter H. Smith, *Politics and Beef in Argentina: Patterns of Conflict and Change* (New York: Columbia Univ. Press, 1969).

11. A good bibliography for economic topics is that of R. Conde and S. Stein, *Latin America. A Guide to Economic History, 1830–1930* (Berkeley: Univ. of California Press, 1977). For an overview, see Roberto Cortes Conde, *The First Stages of Modernization in Spanish America* (New York: Harper and Row, 1974) and Celso Furtado, *Economic Development of Latin America* (Cambridge: Cambridge Univ. Press, 1977). For Argentina, see Carlos Diaz Alejandro, *Essays on the Economic History of the Argentine Republic* (New Haven, Conn.: Yale Univ. Press, 1970); G. Di Tella and R. Dornbusch, *The Political Economy of Argentina, 1946–1983* (Pittsburgh: Univ. of Pittsburgh Press, 1989); and Jonathan Brown, *A Socio-economic History of Argentina, 1776–1860* (Cambridge: Cambridge Univ. Press, 1979). For Brazil, see Thomas W. Merrick and Douglas H. Graham, *Population and Economic Development in Brazil: 1800 to the Present* (Baltimore: Johns Hopkins Univ. Press, 1979) and Werner Baer, *The Brazilian Economy: Growth and Development* (New York: Praeger, 1983). For Mexico, see Clark Reynolds, *The Mexican Economy: Twentieth-Century Structure and Growth* (New Haven, Conn.: Yale Univ. Press, 1970) and Steven Haber, *Industry and Underdevelopment: The Industrialization of Mexico* (Stanford: Stanford Univ. Press, 1989). For Chile, see Markos Mamalakis, *The Growth and Structure of the Chilean Economy* (New Haven, Conn.: Yale Univ. Press, 1976). For some of the Andean nations,

see Paul Gootenberg, *Between Silver and Guano* (Princeton: Princeton Univ. Press, 1991); Rosemary Thorp and Geoffrey Bertram, *Peru 1890–1977: Growth and Policy in an Open Economy* (New York: Columbia Univ. Press, 1978); and Linda Rodriguez, *The Search for Public Policy: Regional Politics and Government Finances in Ecuador, 1830–1940* (Berkeley: Univ. of California Press, 1985). On oil, see John Wirth, *Latin American Oil Companies and the Politics of Energy* (Lincoln: Univ. of Nebraska Press, 1985) and Jonathan Brown, *Oil and Revolution in Mexico* (Berkeley: Univ. of California Press, 1993).

Making Latin American History
Part of the Curriculum

Susan Shapiro ◆ October 1989

In the ten years since I wrote this piece for Perspectives, *I have pursued an approach to early world history study that enables students to examine differences and similarities between development in the Eastern and Western hemispheres. I dutifully provide a variety of materials and perspectives from which students may form judgments about the history of East versus West. The unit is becoming stronger each time I teach it, but something has been still lacking there.*

The best solution I found is in teaching an elective course on modern Latin American history that enables students to pursue the topic in earnest. The course is one quarter long (approximately ten weeks), and we study Latin America not as a single chronological entity, but in chronological/regional/cultural order. We read history texts, but we also read novellas and short stories, listen to music, and visit museums. Students are required to learn a base of material about the whole of the region, but then are assigned to a country or area for in-depth analysis. They become representatives from that country or region. This enables a more substantial discussion, for example, of the impact of caudillismo *in Mexico as compared with Venezuela. Students develop both understanding and attachments through a kind of advocacy. I hope that the understanding and attachment will last well past the course.*

◆　◆　◆　◆

An unwritten law of teaching is that we must find a way to reach every child in our classes. Last year my bag of tricks didn't have anything for Juan (fictitious name). I quickly realized that I had no tools to break through his recalcitrance, his aloofness. No amount of encouragement, no appeal to his need for academic help worked. I didn't understand him or from where he had come. He understood that better than I.

It is no surprise that I should be so ignorant. Most of us had woefully deficient instruction in Latin American history and culture, even though nationally Hispanics now account for 7.9 percent of our population and are its fastest growing segment. Now more than ever the experiences of nations and people in Central and South America require our attention. Pedagogically we cannot ignore such a significant part of our world; we must prepare our students with the tools for intelligent analysis of the problems that face the Americas today.

Even in our small community we have seen significantly more children of Hispanic heritage in our classes. These children are a welcome addition to the cultural diversity of our school, and the beauty and uniqueness of their ethnic heritage is as important as those traditionally acknowledged and supported. But we as teachers need to be aware of familial and cultural factors distinct from our mainstream cultures that may inhibit or enhance a Hispanic child's experience in school. We need to be informed, but how?

The very terms "Hispanic" and "Latino" present a problem for understanding Latin American culture. They leave an impression that there is one dominating culture that exists south of the Rio Grande. In truth, the history and experiences of each nation south of the United States border make for a different blend of characteristics that prevent easy generalizations.

Realization of my professional impotence in dealing with children such as Juan only highlighted the problem I had in developing the new curriculum for an early world history class at the ninth-grade level. If world history is not only the history of the Eastern Hemisphere, *what* needs to be examined in the Western? Where and how should students read, study, know about the West? And, initially, what should the teacher read, study, and know about the West?

The premise of this new first-year course is that the complexities of the modern world can be better understood if we examine the breadth and diversity of human experience in ancient times. Using a model for examining culture, we study the development of each civilization as it moves toward modernity. Religion, in particular, plays an important role in our study of evolving cultures. Students move toward an increasingly sophisticated and sensitive understanding of the people who make up our pluralistic world, even our classrooms. How does the history of the Americas fit into the model, and does it?

I resolved my immediate concern (general ignorance of the Hispanic world) by applying for and receiving a fellowship to study Latin American history at Loyola University during the summer. The program allowed me and fourteen others to study intensively the history and development of Central and South America through monthly meetings, guest speaker presentations, and ongoing discussion of pertinent issues in Latin America today. For example, our October speaker, Tom Sheehan, from the department of philosophy, Loyola University of Chicago, gave an extraordinary presentation on the situation in El Salvador. Professor Sheehan is also a freelance journalist and writer on Central American affairs.

Questions about the nature and extent of coverage of hispanic history and culture still remain, but I now have some ideas about what is important to know—for example, simple histories, differences and similarities, changes over time, transference to North America, etc. Much is left undone. I do look forward to grappling with the rest of the task.

Teaching India in a World History Survey

Tara Sethia ◆ March 1996

Ever since the appearance of this article in Perspectives, *I have received comments from colleagues and friends from all over. Based on my reflections, I have made minor revisions and have updated the article in terms of new resources. Here, I would like to add the following web sites that my students have found very useful. Like other sources, the use of Internet sites, too, benefits from critical discussion. See India: http://www.indiagov.org and SARAI: http://www.columbia.edu/cu/libraries/indiv/area/sarai.*

◆　◆　◆　◆

India represents a core Asian tradition as well as one of the oldest strands in the fabric of world civilization. Indian religions, philosophies, art, literature, and social systems have played a fundamental role in defining the human heritage, and they merit a proper discussion in a world history survey.

Historically, India, like China, has been a seminal influence on the societies and cultures of Asia. People of the Himalayan regions, Sri Lanka, and a large part of Southeast Asia have been greatly affected by Indian culture. Buddhism, originating in India, became—and still remains—a dominant religion in several Asian countries, including China and Japan. India has also influenced the making of the modern world: Indian inventions and innovations in science, medicine, and mathematics contributed to the emergence of these disciplines. For example, the Indian discovery of zero and numerals, mistakenly referred to as Arabic numerals, revolutionized mathematical knowledge.

Traditionally, Indian raw materials have been attractive to the West just as the subcontinent has been a vast market for industrial goods. And today, India is poised to become a major exporter of value-added goods and services. Hence, the study of Indian society is intrinsically important for understanding the rest of Asia and is relevant as well to a historical understanding of the emergence of the modern world.

From a more contemporary perspective, India is the world's largest democracy and a leading developing country. Its population—representing more than 950 million people of diverse cultures, languages, religions, and food habits—continues to be a growing attraction to the consumer and labor-oriented industries of the West.

The distinctiveness of Indian civilization lies not merely in its antiquity but, more importantly, in its continuity and diversity. Hindus, for example, continue to seek inspiration from traditions and concepts similar to those originally advanced by their ancestors. The *Ramayana* and the *Mahabharata*, the epics composed in ancient times, are still read and revered. In the same way, social institutions, languages, and literature show strong trends of continuity. This, however, does not mean that Indian society has been static. In fact, it is important to note that Indian traditions have constantly evolved over the past three and a half millennia. And Indian society is perplexingly multicultural, multiethnic, multilingual, and multireligious, though officially a secular state.

AN APPROACH TO TEACHING INDIA IN WORLD HISTORY

Given such longevity and diversity, teaching about the Indian subcontinent can be both a fascinating and a frustrating experience. And, teaching about India in a world history course poses additional challenges. India has continued to be imagined and imaged in diverse ways by scholars and laypeople alike. For instance, in the past India was seen by some as the land of the maharajas, and by others as a home of snake charmers. At one time perceived as a source of fabulous and untold wealth, India today is seen as a land of abject poverty. As in the past, India continues to be associated with spirituality, metaphysical reality, mystical happenings, and the sacred cow. While some continue to romanticize and idealize the image of India, others look on it with contempt and disdain. For some, India evokes the memories of Gandhi; for others, that of the *Raj*. While contemporary India is seen by many as a land plagued with poverty and communal conflict, it is viewed by many others as a nation equipped with several sophisticated technologies of the twenty-first century. Thus, the challenge in teaching about India lies not so much in providing basic knowledge about India, but rather in exposing students to the connections between the images and the realities that have characterized Indian society from antiquity to the present, and in enabling students to see India as a land of unity in diversity, of tradition and modernity, and of change and continuity.

There is also the challenge of time. How much time (measurable in class periods) should be devoted to the discussion of the Indian subcontinent in a world history survey? Related to the question of time is that of topics: what to discuss and what to discard? Equally important are concerns about the extent of depth and detail. And there is the difficulty of how to communicate concepts that are completely foreign to many students.

While it is difficult to arrive at specific answers to these questions and problems, it is possible to address them within the context of the general structure of and approach to the teaching of world history. If a teacher takes an integrated approach to world history, for instance, it will be hard to measure time to be spent on a specific culture in terms of class periods, just as the question of depth and detail might be subject to a given level of student-teacher interest. I emphasize a comparative approach to the study of various traditional and contemporary societies in a world historical context. This format has several advantages. It engages students in a meaningful intellectual exercise that requires them to identify the unique qualities characteristic of an individual civilization while allowing them to grasp more effectively the similarities among civilizations. This approach also enables students to focus on the larger issues and trends that characterize human history and helps to broaden their perspectives. The themes selected for discussion in this paper are not prescriptive but, rather, represent some of the broader issues in a world historical context.

As I begin to teach about India, I usually ask students to share their images of the subcontinent. This brief but informal dialogue helps me to understand how the students have come to acquire their impressions (for example, through films, novels, newspapers, television, personal contact, or academic training). I then use this context to discuss the diverse range of scholarly and popular views about Indian society and to raise key issues related to the subject, such as the influence of dominant discourse in shaping images about other cultures. For instance, I explain how the Orientalist discourse (see Edward Said, *Orientalism*), has shaped Western images about the "Orient" and "Orientals."

LAND AND PEOPLE

A discussion of "imaginative" geography and culture explicit in terms such as "Orient" and "Orientals" is then juxtaposed with a discussion of my first important theme, the land and peoples of India. This theme allows the class to examine India's specific place in world geography, especially on the Asian land mass, and the influence of geographical features on its history and culture. The theme provides students with a thorough orientation to India's unique physical features and helps them understand how these features shaped the country's history. A brief discussion of the cultural geography of India exposes students to its numerous languages, dialects, and complex cultural contours. Time permitting, I have students (in groups) do a short class exercise of mapping India (that is, identifying by marking on a blank map the major features of the physical and cultural geography of the subcontinent), using historical atlases and wall maps. I conclude the discussion of the theme by fleshing out the connection between geography and history. I examine how, for example, the Himalayas and monsoons have historically affected the people of the subcontinent. Teachers will find Joseph Schwartzberg, ed., *A Historical Atlas of South Asia* a good reference to consult.

The connection between geography and history can be further extended by a discussion of Indus Valley civilization in the global context of riverine civilizations, the growth and diffusion of agriculture and farming techniques, and the rise of urban trends from the dawn of history. This discussion sets the context for a comparative study of the river-based civilizations of the ancient world. It enables students to perceive similarities and differences underlying human heritage across the globe. They learn to identify the common characteristics of river-based civilizations flourishing in the Euphrates-Tigris valleys, the Indus River valley, the Nile River valley, and the Yellow River valley while appreciating the distinctive and unique characteristics of each. For example, in discussing the geographic extent of these civilizations, it can be pointed out that the Harappan (or Indus valley) civilization, which encompassed 840,000 square miles, was probably twice the size of the old kingdom of Egypt and four times that of Sumer and Akkad. Or, the connectedness of civilizations and peoples of the ancient world might be illustrated by focusing on evidence of Indian contact with the civilizations to the west. For example, the commercial contacts with the Euphrates-Tigris civilization can be demonstrated by archaeological evidence pointing to Harappan manufactures found in Mesopotamia.

The migration and movement of people, including nomadic invasions, played a significant role in defining the cultural, ethnic, and racial contours of the ancient world. In the large context of the migration of Indo-Europeans, I introduce the coming of Indo-Aryans to the Indian subcontinent. The ensuing interaction between the nomadic Indo-Aryans, equipped with horse-driven chariots, and the highly cultured people of the Indus valley lays the groundwork for the Vedic age, the second stage of civilization in India (around 1500 B.C.E.). Relying on the evidence from philology and archaeology, a majority of scholars maintain that the Aryan tribes were part of the Indo-Europeans who originated somewhere in central Asia or southern Russia. These people migrated in constant waves toward Europe and India. It is interesting to note that although Indo-Aryans and Greeks came from the same stock of people (that is, the Indo-Europeans), they met as strangers in the sixth-century B.C.E. Persian empire. The characteristics of the Greek and Aryan gods in regulating the order of nature and in banishing evil from the world can be highlighted to show their common background and heritage. However, it is important to point out that the so-called Vedic culture and civilization owed its origin not only to the Indo-Aryans, but, as recent research suggests, also to an amalgam of Aryan and Harappan cultures. (For details about key issues and controversies pertaining to the representation of ancient Indian history, see Romila Thapar's *Interpreting Early India*.)

The Emergence of Traditions: Hinduism, Jainism, and Buddhism

Students can be familiarized briefly with the sources of Indian traditions—the Vedic and the epic literature. Focusing on selected excerpts from *Rig Veda* (see Ainslie T. Embree, ed., *Sources of Indian Tradition*, vol. 1), one of the most ancient surviving pieces of literature, I ask students to discuss the cosmology and worldview that characterize the Indian tradition as well as the role of ritual and sacrifice. This discussion can be carried further with more concrete examples of Indian tradition and values drawn from the two epics, *Ramayana* and *Mahabharata*. However, it is important to discuss these epics in the context of "Great Traditions" versus "Little Traditions." The discussion of epics representing the great traditions may be balanced with the inclusion of select folktales from India representing the little traditions. The folktales not only offer valuable insights to compare with those from the epics but also reveal the diversity of the folk traditions in Indian culture, and when combined with the discussion of epics help students to understand that no culture or tradition should be understood as a monolith. Moreover, the students love to read and discuss folktales. (See R. K. Ramanujan, ed., *Folk Tales from India*.) This discussion can also be used to show the evolving nature of traditions, which shows traditions as examples of both continuity and change. A documentary film, *Great Tales in Asian Art*, vividly reveals through the media of art, architecture, dance, music, painting, and theater the enduring nature of Indian and some other Asian traditions.

The way is now paved for a more specific discussion of the evolution of Hinduism, Jainism, and Buddhism in the historical context of the evolution of religious and philosophical traditions in the ancient world. Taking Hinduism as a case in point, I ask, What is Hinduism? Is it a religion or a philosophy? Is it earthly or metaphysical? Is it spiritual or material? Is it polytheistic or monotheistic? Is it a social practice or a complete way of life?

The discussion of Buddhism and Jainism can be used to stimulate comparative and global thinking. I also focus on how, for example, Jainism and Buddhism emerged in India in the context of changing socioreligious trends, and why Jainism remained totally inside India while Buddhism spread beyond the Indian subcontinent. The spread of Buddhism from India can be used to illustrate the connectedness of world regions during ancient times. At the same time, one can raise a question about how Buddhism posed a challenge to Hindu society during the classical period in India just as it did to the Confucian state in China. This context enables me to come back to the subcontinent and examine the changes that took place in classical (or Gupta) India, as well as to flesh out the evolutionary nature of Hinduism, by pointing out how and why Hinduism assumed the shape that it did. This can be explained by reference to the prescribed Four Ends of Man (Dharma, Artha, Kama, and Moksha) and to the Four Stages of Human Life (the Four Ashramas: Brhmacharya, Grihastha, Vanaprastha, and Sanyasa). This explanation enables students to see that Hinduism is more than just a religion or social practice, that it is a complete way of life—spiritual and material.

A related issue in this context is the relation of these religious systems to Indian social structures. Using excerpts from the Bhagvad Gita and the Dhammapada, we examine the connection between religious and moral imperatives and evolving social and political structures. Here, the Hindu sanction for social behavior (for example, the Four Ends of Man, the Four Ashramas), as illustrated in the Gita, can be compared to the Buddhist sense of righteousness and duty, as illustrated in the Dhammapada. In addition to examining the role of social codes and religious sanctions, it is useful to reflect on the role and place of the individual and the family in the larger social and political structure, since a majority of our students are completely unfamiliar with social systems different from their own. Ideas of order and harmony can be examined with reference to the Varna (caste) system as an organizing principle in the social structure. It is, however, important to note the rigid as well as flexible nature of the caste system. For example, the founder of the first imperial age in India, Chandragupta Maurya, was not of the khshatriya caste (second from the top in social hierarchy and traditionally the caste of the rulers and warriors), but of the vaishya caste (second from the bottom, the caste of the merchants and artisans).

At the same time, the plurality of Indian traditions and their respective social and political influence can be highlighted by a discussion of the role of Jainism and Buddhism (which also represented resistance to Brahmanic authority under Hinduism and were therefore anticaste in nature) in shaping the Mauryan state in India. The classic examples are Chandragupta, founder of the Mauryan state, who renounced the world by becoming a Jain monk, and his grandson, Asoka the Great, whose polity and life were deeply influenced by Buddhism.

The global theme of the ancient empires can be used as a context to discuss the rise of Magadha, the Mauryan empire, India's first imperial unification, and the Gupta empire, the classical period of Indian history.

This theme allows the teacher to demonstrate the interconnectedness of history through a discussion of empires and imperial expansion elsewhere in the ancient world. In this context, Alexander the Great's Indian expedition, just before the rise of the Mauryas, can be highlighted to point out that he was accompanied by a number of Hellenistic scholars whose purpose was to acquire knowledge about the ideas and religions of India. His staff also surveyed roads in Asia, which led to increased commercial and cultural interaction. The Mauryan king, Chandragupta Maurya, maintained close diplomatic relations with the Hellenistic kingdom. Trade with India dominated the commercial and trading relations of the Roman empire. Egypt was a valuable link between the trading worlds of the Indian Ocean and the Mediterranean.

INDIA AND THE ARAB WORLD

Contact between India and the Arab world, although starting earlier, became more pronounced and significant during the medieval period. The long-established trade between the Persian Gulf and the Indian Ocean became a subject of several notable Arabic works. The Arabs appear to have had high regard for India. Saif-i-Hindi (the Indian sword) was their favorite weapon. Arab interest in India is also attested by the records of numerous Arab travelers, ranging from Sulaiman the merchant to the globe-trotter Ibn Battuta. Indians were seen as "men unsurpassed in science, especially astronomy." The period between 500 and 800 was indeed remarkable for scientific activity in India, especially in astronomy and mathematics. For a long time it was believed in Europe that the symbol for zero and the decimal system of notations were of Arab origin (thus the misnomer, Arabic numerals), but it is now universally acknowledged that these passed from India to Europe through the Arabs.

The rise and expansion of Islam is a major theme for medieval world history. In this context several important questions can be raised about the advent of Islam in India. Why was the coming of Islam delayed until the tenth century, especially given historical contacts between Arabia and India? Who were the people who brought Islam to India? Why did Islam come to India not through Arabia but via the Khyber pass—a strategic passage for all invaders of India from the northwest? These questions set a comparative context and allow students to grasp what was different or unique about the Islamic onslaught in India, and how it paved the way for the establishment of the Mughal empire and a distinct Islamic art, architecture, and culture in the subcontinent. K. N. Chaudhuri's *Asia Before Europe: Economy and Civilization of the Indian Ocean from the Rise of Islam to 1750* is an insightful and useful scholarly reference.

The Indian case can be compared, for example, to that of China. Both experienced invasions from the northwest between 1000 and 1300, and both cultures survived these major interventions. In India, despite several centuries of Muslim rule, Hinduism remained intact as a majority religion. Islam imbibed many cultural traits of Hinduism and vice versa. Such an exchange created change as well as synthesis. A comparative analysis of the Bhakti and Sufi movements reveals the sharing of certain common characteristics. For example, both movements aimed at unity with God through love and devotion; challenged the traditional guardians of religions, the Pundits and the Ulama; recognized the significance of guru and the pir; advocated the use of vernacular languages; appealed largely to the lower classes; and led to the fusion of cultures. An examination of selected excerpts from these movements (drawn from *Sources of Indian Tradition*, vol. 1) provides an instructive introduction to these cultural movements, and lends a different perspective to the interaction between Islam and Hinduism—one based on mutual respect, sharing, and caring.

While Buddhism was eliminated from its original homeland, the early medieval period witnessed its spread throughout central Asia, Tibet, Nepal, China, Korea, Japan, and parts of southeast Asia. It was also from India that Islam spread to Southeast Asia. (Similarly the Mongol invasions of Asian land masses led to the spread of Chinese inventions, especially gunpowder and the compass, which helped Europeans to launch what became known as the Age of Exploration.) Once again, the movement of people and ideas allows students to see the interconnectedness of history.

The Mughal empire in India can be used to discuss a model of empire different from the European colonial empires. The Mughals, as patrons of art, architecture, and paintings left monumental legacies such as the Taj Mahal, which continue to remain as highly distinctive features of India today. Slides of Mughal art and architecture, a taste of north Indian cuisine, and Hindustani music can help emphasize the syncretic attributes of Mughal art, architecture, and culture as a whole.

EUROPEAN IMPERIALISM

The growth of transoceanic trade, with spices as its focus, allows us to understand the early encounters between Indians and Europeans. It is important to point out, however, that Europeans were peripheral to Asia prior to the nineteenth century. During the eighteenth century a more dominant trend was the revival and reform of tradition in India. Excerpts from social reform movements (see Stephen Hay, ed., *Sources of Indian Tradition*, vol. 2) could be used to assess the nature of indigenous society, culture, and reform on the eve of British political intrusions into the Indian subcontinent. This discussion is particularly meaningful for understanding the images the West had of non-Western people, and vice versa, especially for considering notions of the "barbaric" and the "civilized."

Early European intrusions were primarily characterized by missionary and commercial activities in India and around the Indian Ocean. The multifaceted theme of culture and colonialism can be examined by focusing on the role played by technology in shaping the subsequent interaction between the British and the Indians. This provides a context to understand the rise of Western domination of non-Western regions and peoples. Selected portions of Daniel R. Headrick's *Tools of Empire* are useful in facilitating a broader understanding among students of the subjugation of the highly sophisticated and relatively vast civilization of India by the numerically insignificant British. For example, one can illustrate how railways in nineteenth-century India were used more as tools of imperial expansion and consolidation rather than as means of industrialization and social transformation. By focusing on the agents, missionaries, and trading corporations, such as the British East India Company, it is easy to define and distinguish various brands of imperialism: cultural, political, and economic. Similarly, the case of opium production in colonial India by the British to promote the illegal opium market in China and to get Chinese tea for the British market can help highlight the complex nature of Western imperialism, which manifested itself in different forms and led to a variety of interactions between the colonizers and the colonized. The subtleties of the nature and impact of imperialism can be demonstrated through a discussion of such novels as R. K. Narayan's *The English Teacher* or George Orwell's *Burmese Days*.

Due to centuries of British colonial rule, India also serves as an interesting case study to understand the connection between colonialism and development. Students can examine this through a debate on the subject among the British colonial officials, the Indian nationalists, and the more recent scholars on the subject. (A precise representation of such diverse views on the subject can be found in an article by Bipan Chandra, "Colonial India: British versus Indian Views of Development," *Review* [winter 1991], 81–167.) The discussion of this topic will prepare students better to understand the rise of nationalism in India.

NATIONALISM AND INDEPENDENCE MOVEMENTS: INDIA AND PAKISTAN

Just as imperialism was a global trend of the nineteenth century, so also nationalism and independence movements characterized the world of the late nineteenth and twentieth centuries. The various strands of the nationalist movement in India and its diverse leadership can be illustrated through a discussion of excerpts from primary source documents (for example, *Sources of Indian Tradition*, vol. 2). The discussion may be further accentuated by exposing students to the literature of national awakening, such as Munshi Prem Chand's *Selected Short Stories*, and by critically integrating discussion of films such as *Bharat ki Khoj* (literally meaning "search of the Indian nation"). Questions about the role of leaders versus masses in the transformation of history and historical change can be explored by focusing on a novel by R. K. Narayan, *Waiting for the Mahatma* or on Raja Rao's *Kanthapura*. Either novel might be juxtaposed with Shahid Amin's essay "Gandhi as Mahatma" (in Ranajit Guha and Gayatri C. Spivak, eds., *Selected Subaltern Studies*), and the film *Gandhi*. The peculiarities of Indian nationalism can be highlighted by raising and examining the question of why the national movement in India resulted in the creation of two nations: India and Pakistan. Thus, nationalism can also be discussed to understand the phenomenon of partition in India, which was as much nationalistic as it was political. Select clips from a recent documentary can help accentuate the impact of partition of the ordinary people of India who were not consulted about partition, but merely became victims of partition resulting from politics in colonial India. (See *Division of Hearts*, with English subtitles, directed and produced by Satti Khanna.) India played a leading role in the national and independence movement in Asia, and was the first country after the Philippines to become independent.

In the post-World War II period, the major problems confronting the world have been the problems of democracy and development. In the context of this large and complex theme, India again can be integrated effectively into world history. India is both the largest democracy in the world and a leading developing country. This, however, does not mean there are no challenges to the healthy survival of democracy or to the country's continuous economic development. In fact, the rise of fundamentalism—which is a global phenomenon—has posed serious challenges to the survival of Indian democracy. This theme can be fleshed out with the showing of relevant clips from a highly thought-provoking documentary, *In the Name of God*, directed and produced by Anand Patwardhan. Moreover, the problems of poverty, population, and environmental hazards have inhibited the full realization of developmental benefits. Here India can be compared to the leading developing countries in terms of the continuing interaction between modernity and tradition. Comparisons could focus on the role of authority versus democratic institutions or on issues of poverty and population.

THE WORLD TODAY

It is useful, from the point of view of students, to explain what India is like today. This can be done through a discussion of a variety of issues, including religion, science, theater, film, literature, and the role of women and children. Teachers will find a valuable resource on contemporary India in a special issue of *Daedalus* (1989) entitled *Another India*. This issue includes brief but insightful assessments of present-day realities by some of the leading Indian intellectuals. Also useful and easy to follow are Sara Mitter's *Dharma's Daughters* and the film

Kamala and Raji (with English subtitles, directed and produced by Michael Camerine) for insights into the traditional and changing role of women in India today.

A country with a rich tradition of spiritual masters, India is today rapidly becoming, among other things, a land of software mavens. In a recent commentary in the *Los Angeles Times,* Jonathan Power observed, "In Aesop's fable of the tortoise and the hare, we read one of life's repeating stories: plodding wins the race. I venture to say, by the year 2000 we'll learn this lesson again. It will be India, and not China, that will be on its way to becoming the giant of Asia and, before too much time is past, the largest economy in the world" (*Los Angeles Times,* March 20, 1994, M5). A study of India in world history survey courses is not only vital to understanding of our human heritage, it is also critical to comprehending the twenty-first-century world.

Teaching the United States in World History

Peter N. Stearns ◆ April 1989

The discussion of fitting United States and world history together gains continued momentum, as world history itself picks up momentum. The connections are vital both analytically and in terms of sequencing in history teaching. While discussion gains vigor, concrete steps are still limited. Notably, there remains a distressing dearth of materials that will help teachers make connections, either in the U.S. or the world history survey. More encouraging are a number of high school programs that are staking out imaginative integrations of the two subject areas in a coordinated sequence. We need to learn about these programs and their success, and build on this degree of daring.

The focus of the following remarks, written from a world history standpoint but applicable to U.S. survey connections as well, continues in my judgment to be useful. Emphasize U.S. involvement in larger world patterns such as the world economy, and use this as a base for varied comparisons; confront exceptionalism head-on in a comparative civilizations context, encouraging debate; and deal with the growing importance of the United States in world affairs from the 1860s onward not simply in descriptive fashion, but through another comparative challenge, about what the United States has brought to world history, if anything, that differs from previous West European impacts. I would add the importance of dealing with exceptionalism not only concerning European history, but also the history of other, contemporaneous fron-

tier societies. And I would emphasize, in terms of impact, the desirability of exploring and explaining the extraordinary American role in devising and disseminating mass consumer culture—perhaps (alas) our most marked international innovation.

◆　◆　◆　◆

The dilemma is obvious, visible in most history texts and in all but the most experimental curricula: the past is divided into two parts, the United States and whatever else in the world is studied historically or, more simply and obviously, US and THEM. We can modestly rejoice of course, that there is often something beyond the national horizon, as against some teaching traditions that pay little attention to anything save the glories of one's own country and its antecedents (a narrowness true in some school systems here as well). The fact remains that the characteristic split, between purely United States courses and a world or something-else-course, not only leaves bridges unbuilt but fosters in many students a truly unfortunate tendency toward historical isolationism, as the complexities and troubles of most of the world's history seem oddly unrelated to the glorious saga of our own ascent.

Students do absorb from school and from the general culture a number of myths and half-truths about America's uniqueness and its separation from most larger world processes. They can discuss these in some detail, despite their ignorance about all sorts of United States history specifics and despite considerable cynicism and intelligence in other respects. It is perpetually amazing to me how many good college freshmen know for certain that the United States has historically offered unparalleled mobility opportunities, unprecedented openness to change and progress, and unique altruism in foreign affairs (this last with specific subsets such as the fact that we "gave" the industrial revolution to Japan after World War II, a hardy perennial in my world history courses until I took firmer steps to hammer home the Meiji era).

The fact that beliefs of this sort are oversimple, verging on outright incorrect, in situating the United States in a larger world and comparative framework, suggests a serious task for world historians in helping students locate what they know or think they know about their own national past in a more general history. For students' beliefs affect not only their perceptions of the United States, but a tendency to downgrade other societies because of an implicit impulse to measure these societies against an unrealistically demanding standard. It is probably true, as Leften Stavrianos has argued, that the United States has been unusually lucky in its past, compared to other societies, though even this cannot apply to all key groups in American history, but it has obviously not exceeded world norms so blithely as many students—including students who do very well in world history per se—continue to believe.

The task of addressing these issues, of finding ways to integrate the United States to some degree into world history courses, is at least as formidable as it is compelling. World history courses almost by definition have too much to do already. At the same time the habit of assuming that students "get" their United States history in repetitious abundance, and certainly in separate courses in school and college, remains deeply ingrained. It has been undeniably convenient to let the twain not meet, given the traditions of history teaching and the burdens on those of us who foolhardily present the whole rest of the world in a semester or two. Yet the result has been to leave the task of connecting—or more commonly, of failing to connect—to students themselves. This is a conceptually demanding job, when a world history framework is juxtaposed to a usually rigorously national context presented additionally in a separate course taken in a different year. The task is complicated further, as I have suggested, by the biases many students bring to it. The result, in my firm belief, is a need to do more to provide some suggestive guidance to the process of integration, so that students do not emerge with prejudices unchallenged or simply with the sense that God decreed two different histories, one ours and one theirs.

Having said this, admittedly a fairly obvious point save for our curricular traditions, I have no magic formulas that will make the resulting integration easier. I do have some ideas that may stimulate other suggestions and actual curricular experiments, plus further knowledge of experiments already undertaken. The goal, certainly, should be clear: the need to deal with what seems to me a significant challenge in history teaching now that a world framework is increasingly envisaged.

The challenge does not add up to a need to handle a great deal of narrative detail about American history in the world history course. There is no time, and hopefully, given the possibility of cross-referencing to previous work at least in a college-level course, some limits to the necessity. The desirability of sketching key themes in the United States' past, however, and tying them into the world history framework may seem still more difficult than simply designating a few weeks' chunk to American details. It is this approach, however, that I wish particularly to address, not again with complete plans but with some thoughts on how to proceed.

The first distinction is chronological: the issue of handling American history before the 1870s differs markedly from that afterward. While the North American colonies and the new United States were not without some economic, demographic, and symbolic significance in the wider world before 1870, these points of contact can be fairly quickly evoked and are readily outstripped by the impact of most other inhabited areas including Latin America. After about 1870 this situation changes, among other things as a result of the growing worldscale operations of American agriculture and key corporations such as the Singer sewing machine company. The familiar world political role, becoming visible by the 1890s, followed close on the heels of these earlier contacts and ushered in the overt world power impact with which we still live today, for better or worse. For a world history course that pays serious attention to the later nineteenth and twentieth centuries, then, the claim of United States history for a treatment in detail comparable to that lavished on other major societies, qualified only by a hope of greater student knowledge, is considerable. The suggestion is, then, for a chronological shifting of gears between very broad-brush treatment from the seventeenth to the later nineteenth century, and more meticulous integration over the past 100 years, based on a change in world significance that can be explicitly presented and justified to a world history class.

While detail is not required for world history purposes, the first long period of United States-in-a-wider-world history should not be entirely neglected. It does help illustrate some themes in world history from the seventeenth century onward, as will be suggested below. It is essential as the basis for understanding later United States patterns when world significance cannot be gainsaid. Just as some sketch, albeit brief, must be offered for Russia before 1480, or Japan before and during civilization's initial advent, not for their own sake so much as in order to set some themes that persist into later periods when the societies occupy a more visible place on a world stage, so a formative United States period—if a long one—should not be entirely ignored. And this is all the more important in that student awareness and some common misconceptions begin to apply to this period, making it essential to establish some links to wider themes even before United States inclusion becomes imperative in world terms outright.

Given inherent lack of time and the need not to exaggerate American themes while paying them some heed, the first three centuries of what became United States history must obviously be inserted in a careful analytical framework, not rehearsed in a narrative for its own sake; and this analytical framework is most logically comparative. Some ingredients of North American history may of course have been developed in discussions of Amerindian societies and the European voyages of discovery; I do not mean that focus on 1600 and after has no preparation. In this treatment, however, the principle contributions of a world history framework are, first, to help students see how landmarks of what became United States history fit into larger world trends in this timespan and, second, to locate major features of this history in a comparative context.

The world history course provides an opportunity to ask students—and most of them have never really been presented with questions—what aspects of emerging United States history are truly distinctive, in a comparative framework, and whether indeed the United States was building toward becoming a "civilization" in its own right. Of course the debate about American exceptionalism needs to be framed with care, lest it escape the proper time limitations of a world history course and take on undue significance. In a course, though, that builds on a civilizations approach to some degree, and has already established the importance of careful comparison as one means of gaining intelligibility and managing data, these basic questions about early United States history follow logically. They also allow, again if only briefly, some treatment of certain of the common student misconceptions. I spend at least one session, and it is usually a lively one, talking about the American exceptionalist argument particularly as it applies before 1900. I want students to know in capsule form the latest findings about comparative mobility patterns, which indicate that American mobility culture differed from that of other frontier or early-industrial societies considerably more than the reality of mobility differed, and what this all means about the way we conceive of the United States' past in larger comparative terms. I want them to remember that key distinctive ingredients of the United States' past, such as the importance and some unusual characteristics of slavery, do not fit easily into the most conventional God-bless-America comparative framework.

And for my purposes, in a short and highly thematic world history course, I want students to see that for the most part the United States can be grasped as an extension of Western civilization. This is not, I admit to them, an incontestable choice. American exceptionalism has some valid as well as exaggerated bases in fact, even if established on carefully comparative ground rather than—as is the wont of most Americanists themselves—merely asserted. Students should acknowledge some ingredients here, as in racial and frontier issues (including proclivity to violence and relatively weak government controls), or religion and family patterns that began to take shape as early as the seventeenth century. It might be desirable, where time permits, to develop a larger civilizational category that would embrace the United States, Canada, Australia, and New Zealand, admitting close connections to Western civilization but emphasizing distinguishing experiences, not all of which, however, were those of the United States alone.

But I try to defend the extension of Western civilization hypothesis, arguing indeed that there are fewer problems integrating United States history into modern Western history than there are in treating Japan as part of a Chinese-inspired East Asian civilization, a comparative civilizations problem with which my course has grappled earlier. (Indeed, an essay assignment on precisely this topic has worked rather well.)

Arguments about shared cultural origins—due reminders offered about non-Western groups in the developing North American population—here blend with the startling degree of chronological parallelism around such trends as the late eighteen-/nineteenth-century demographic transition; the industrial revolution; new sexual behaviors and Victorianisn; more democratic politics (though here with the vital caveat that the United States was unusual, and has seen unusual results, in establishing majority male universal suffrage prior to industrialization rather than afterward, in contrast to most other Western countries).

The exact degree of United States participation in modern Western trends, and key qualifications such as the existence of slavery and its racial aftermath or the unusual persistence of religious belief in the nineteenth and twentieth centuries, must obviously be discussed and treated as interpretive problems rather than a set of tidy historical findings; but its analytical advantages, as well as the issues left dangling, can be indicated in a fairly brief discussion. The claim of shared Western-ness can be further discussed from the vantagepoint of more clearly different societies in the same period of time, including in many respects Latin America, from whose angle of vision the United States as a frontier outpost of the West would seem if anything more obvious than it does to most of us and our students.

With early United States history sketched comparatively, and its civilizational position—or lack of fully separate position—established, it is then possible to show United States participation in key world historical trends in the same three-century span. The simplest aspects involve showing United States inclusion in general Western evolution, through the industrial revolution, the growing fascination with science, and participation in political upheaval. There are, however, crosscutting currents that among other things bring early United States history into different comparative contexts without vitiating (necessarily at least) the basic Western-ness argument.

The place of the North American colonies in Wallerstein's world economy is a case in point that allows contact with some familiar facts about colonial economic dependence. North America was in some sense a peripheral economy, though outside the South a less important and therefore less closely regulated one than Latin America at the same time. Relatively weak government and coercive labor systems established in the seventeenth and eighteenth centuries certainly follow from peripheral status as Wallerstein defines it, and this can in turn (where time permits) serve as framework for more extended comparison of slave systems both in this world economy and in relation to slavery in earlier societies. It is obviously true that to the extent the North American colonies were peripheral, they managed to pull out of this status, into industrialization, unusually rapidly. This may occasion a bit of student boosterism, but it can be explained, while the lingering effects of peripheralism, in the South-North relationship or in the ongoing United States indebtedness through 1914, should also be noted.

A second crosscutting trend context, again shared with Latin America and, later, with many twentieth-century societies, involves new nation status. While students will readily see that the United States avoided some new nations problems that beset Latin America slightly later, they can also see some classic new nations issues in, for example, the Civil War. Furthermore, some ongoing effects of new nations experience, suitably glossed with an exaggerated version of the Western ideology of liberal individualism, showed in the persistent weakness of the American state. Here is a striking United States departure from Western norms until at least the 1930s, and again an interesting similarity to Latin American patterns. I have found the theme increasingly useful as a follow-up to the civilizational comparison, not because it is more important than the world economy determination but because it is more complex. It jolts students more, and usefully. American government weakness, while not a total surprise given anti-statist ideology, deserves some careful statement as against dominant Western trends and despite the tendency of conventional United States history courses to treat the state as central actor from the revolution onward. Rates of crime and vigilantism, compared to Western trends, form one useful illustration. While American political characteristics did touch base with Western (particularly British) political ideology, they also deserve assessment in the light of new nations theory and the concurrent experience of new governments in Latin America.

It is important, obviously, not to chop up the United States patterns into too many discrete fragments. Indication of basic civilizational characteristics, however, can allow crosscutting participation in certain other world patterns where the United States position differed, at least initially, from that of the Western leaders. This in turn amplifies other comparative possibilities and simultaneously shows how world patterns really apply to our own society and not simply to more remote corners of the world where the absence of full historical free will is less surprising and (to most American students) less important, less jarring. The same process, of diverse comparison and insertion in larger world trends and relationships, helps students make United States historical data, new or previously acquired, coherent and assessable in world-historical terms. And, in broad outline at least, depending on student capacity and the level of detail that time permits, it can be sketched fairly economically, precisely because it calls on skills and concepts already utilized in other segments of the world course.

Elements of the same approach obviously can continue in the amplified treatment that becomes desirable from the 1870s onward. The comparative context must be retained. As the United States matured as an industrial society, and as Western Europe shed further vestiges of traditional structures that had never taken root in North America, from peasant agriculture to monarchical government, convergence in key features of the main segments of Western society became a leading theme. Some—though by no means all—of the qualifications necessary in the earlier period, in inserting the United States as part of a large Western civilization, now declined in salience. Indeed, from the 1920s onward the United States took a leadership role in defining many key features of the Western version of advanced industrial society, particularly in the realm of consumerism and popular culture. While political differences remained (indeed widened, in comparing the United States and Britain) during the twentieth century, the new nation limitations on American government waned somewhat and reduced the distinction in state functions.

Obviously, world economy analysis remains useful, as the United States moved more firmly into core status along with the rest of the West (and ultimately Japan).

The principal new theme to handle is of course the United States' ascension to superpower status. This evolution, familiar enough in many ways, can organize this second of the chronological segments devoted to the United States-world interaction, centered of course on the twentieth century rather than the early-modern, industrial decades. Quite apart from the narrative material to adduce—world war roles, emergence from isolation, postwar diplomacy, the rise of multinational corporations—the theme builds on the world economy approach, in linking the more recent articulations of core status to the changing world power balance of which the United States has been a major beneficiary. There is a link too, though a more complex one, to the expanded Western civilization theme set earlier: to what extent did the United States, in gaining new military and diplomatic power, pick up distinctively Western interests and approaches? Tensions between United States-Western affiliations and the actual geography of the United States usefully inform a number of diplomatic trends in the twentieth century and shape some questions about world politics (Pacific vs. Atlantic foci) in the near future. Assessing the United States as a Western imperialist newcomer, though a distinctive one because of twentieth-century world power realities and the revolutionary heritage of the United States itself, is another useful application of earlier comparative efforts to the new world power balance. American diplomatic moralism, plus certain racist themes, obviously evoke Western impulses that were only slightly more blatant a century ago.

At the same time, the United States' world power rise complicates earlier comparisons in important respects. The United States has become, since 1945, more militarized and diplomatically conservative just as much as the West has become somewhat less so. Here, trends are at work that muddy the convergence theme. And superpower status also invites a comparison with the Soviet Union in attributes and goals beneath rhetoric; this comparison, like the new nations analysis in the previous period, may highlight complexities in the United States-as-Western model without necessarily overturning it.

The invitation, then, is to an adapted comparative approach that will build upon the obvious shift in power position over the past century while utilizing the comparative themes sketched a bit earlier in the world history course. This approach allows some extensive narrative passages where time permits. It provides students some opportunity to deal with major changes (including growing attachment to more conservative international interests—from Yankee Doodle to Great Satan in less than ten generations). It also establishes continuities with earlier features of United States society, such as the close relationship to larger Western patterns including now the movement toward a service economy and new immigration streams. It yields, finally, a chance to discuss United States world impact in something more than random fashion, by using themes from the world economy, the new superpower concept and attendant comparison, and assessment of relationships with earlier Western imperialist impulses seen not simply as thrusts toward political or economic domination but also as assertions of cultural hegemony.

Much is not covered in the scheme outlined here, given the emphasis on analytical frameworks rather than staples of the United States history game. There are surely many alternatives to the schema itself, in the whole or in part. Some instructors would doubtless find too much comparative complexity hard to handle for their student clientele and would prefer to limit the vantage points. What I do think can be widely urged, apart from some of the specifics already outlined, boils down to three main points. The first is that the United States should be discussed in the world history course for several good reasons. The second point is that this discussion can be manageable by using comparison, by dividing treatment into two basic chronological segments very simple to define in terms of world power roles, and by hooking into leading world history as the unfolding of basic international economic relationships. The third point is that a variety of frameworks exist by which the inclusion of the United States can fit analytical goals and not involve an occasional, somewhat random narrative stroll through episodes. Frameworks exist, in other words, that can encompass discussion of United States history within other course goals. Furthermore, these frameworks can apply to the United States a rule that I believe must be fundamental in a world history course: societies worth discussing at all must not be simply popped in and out sporadically, but given enough character that major actions, such as diplomatic initiatives, can be interpreted in terms of causation and evaluated in terms of change and continuity in light of past trajectories. The frameworks applied to the United States may be evoked only briefly, for want of time, but a sketch at least is possible, so that students can begin to think of American history as part of a world pattern, in which some of the issues they discern in other societies can be carried over.

There is, then, a need to rethink the United States-world history relationship; the need can be manageably met, though various emphases are possible; and manageability can and should include coherence, not in terms of masses of detail but in terms of one or more analytical frameworks consistently applied.

Four final points must be made beyond these basic assertions. First, any new experiments with greater attention to the United States in world history should assume a certain amount of student obduracy. Beliefs about American separateness—a large if informal adherence to the exceptionalist school—die hard (and of course in some cases, carefully stated, they can be defended). It is easy to be disappointed about how much students can separate one framework of analysis from older habits that will crop up when a new topic or problem is addressed. Without pushing any particular conceptual agenda, it is worth noting that some points about reconceptualizing American history need to be hammered dramatically, if only to open a more questioning outlook.

Second, while good lectures and class discussions are possible around some of the points discussed above, it is obvious that some provocative reading matter that puts the United States into one or more comparative contexts would be a tremendous boon. World history books don't do this, because of their normally unanalytical approach and their particular uncertainty when it comes to United States history. Americanists tend to discourage the approach because of their normally blithe unawareness of comparative issues and possibilities (slavery and maybe why-no-socialism excepted). Some attention to relevant, and suitably brief, teaching materials would be timely, certainly feasible, and potentially a real advance in structuring history curricula.

Third, the task of relating United States and world history should be a two-way street. Without changing all their habits, Americanists should become more alert to the possibility of linking what they teach about to what students have learned or will learn in world history. This means some attention, from the more strictly United States perspective, to comparative issues and larger world trends; it means picking up systematically not only on changes in world power roles but also the impact of international influences on American life. Too much has been written of late about the problems of world history in diverting students from the values of their own society, without dealing with the total history package to which more students are exposed not only in college but in schools. While world historians can take up some responsibility for helping students to see how "our" history fits the world framework, the interchange must be mutual, as Americanists take fuller cognizance of what world history is about and how it bears on what they teach. The compartmentalization that students learn too well in history, which a world history course must attack to some degree, reflects lack of sequenced curricular relationships and, often, a real compartmentalization among historians. World historians must and can learn that their bailiwick is not "everything except the United States." American history teachers can correspondingly learn that one of their themes must be a positioning of United States development amid larger trends.

This leads to the final point, which can return us to the larger world history thrust. Until American history instructors convert to greater utilization of an international and comparative framework, world history teachers may justly fear that inclusion of United States topics will divert from their basic commitment to provide cultural breadth to a stubbornly parochial student body. Some students may indeed rivet on the United States entry into world affairs over the past century, as if this alone provided coherence in a global hodgepodge. This can be guarded against by restricting allocations of class time to reasonable proportions, and by the careful comparisons and application of larger themes already recommended. Focused discussion of the exceptional features of the United States position in the 1950s and 1960s, and the subsequent relative decline explained through a combination of American and world developments, can be a timely corrective. So can some exploration of views of the United States held by other societies, and how these link both to larger cultural diversities and to American behaviors.

Students need not emerge from a sensible presentation with a belief that the United States has become the pivot of world history, though it remains desirable if comparable attention to international influences and constraints, applied to coverage of the twentieth century in United States courses, enhances this message. While risks exist of some lack of proportion, then they can be addressed. The current system, encouraging assumptions about United States-world connections to go almost entirely unexamined, is riskier still. Quite apart from its implications for properly balanced perspective on our own society, it misses opportunities for challenging analysis where students need it most, in seeing the relationships between "their" environment and the past and the wider world to which, happily, history teachers are increasingly trying to expose them.